D1096215

THE QUAKER

THE QUAKER

A Study in Costume

BY

AMELIA MOTT GUMMERE

" Chuse thy Cloaths by thine own eye,
not anothers.   The more simple and plain
they are, the better.   Neither unshapely,
nor fantastical ; and for Use and Decency,
and not for Pride."

WILLIAM PENN, 1693.
" Some Fruits of Solitude."

BENJAMIN BLOM  New York/London 1968

First Published 1901
Reissued 1968
by Benjamin Blom, Inc. Bronx, New York 10452
and 56 Doughty Street London, W.C. 1

Library of Congress Catalog Card Number 68-56494

Printed in the United States of America

INTRODUCTION.

The traditional idea of Quakerism always carries with it a suggestion of peculiarity in dress; and this peculiarity has been so marked, that Quaker life can hardly be portrayed without an understanding of the history of the garb. The day has come, however, when the question of dress, even for the Quaker, is no longer bound up with the plan of salvation. We have him sufficiently in perspective to turn our modern camera upon him, and study the variations of this once vital question; for if it is in any degree true that " dress makes the man," certain it is that dress at one time went far to make a Quaker—at least to the world's thinking. There is a picturesque side to the story of the Quaker; he himself hardly appreciates how much of the romantic there has been in his quiet life. The trend of his thought has led him to take himself too seriously, and he has lost much of the sense of his relation to the great world around him. Quaker dress and customs have varied as the times have changed, often in a very interesting way; but perfect simplicity, uninfluenced by outside thought, is nowhere to be found in this world, short of Patagonia. The student of a philosophic turn of mind will find much light thrown upon the man in drab, if he will attentively observe his habits, manner of life and " conversation "—a word meaning in the Quaker, as in the Pauline vocabulary,

his whole style of living, and intercourse with his fel-
low-men.

There are three distinct periods into which the history of Quaker dress will naturally fall:—the period of
persecution, when the early Friends had everything at
stake, and life was to them more than meat and the
body than raiment; the second, or reactionary period,
when their position was established, their cause won,
and prosperity, with its successes, was proving, as it
always will prove, a far more dangerous foe than the
perils of adversity; and the third, or modern period,
when the crisis of the present brings them face to face
with intricate problems, and dress again falls into its
proper place in the general scheme of things. We shall
see that in the face of a real issue, Quakerism disre-
garded the question of dress; and it is worth while to
trace the growth and development of the traditional
idea of Quaker costume, as it has come to be universally
accepted. In other words, we shall study the Quaker
in the light of a Higher Criticism, applied to the Doctrine of Clothes.

Since the great days of persecution, when, for the
sake of a principle, all the minor " testimonies " gained
in weight and import, bearing their share in forwarding
the cause of Truth and Quakerism, many of the beliefs
then peculiar to a sect are now held by multitudes of
God-fearing people the world over. A total absence in
the denominational schools of any proper teaching of
Quaker history, has in past years made the matter of
dress a veritable " cross " to many a youthful member,
who has thrown off the obnoxious burden as soon as he
was master of his own movements; a result that might

frequently have been avoided, had he at all appreciated his inheritance. But an understanding of the spirit of Quakerism can no more come by heredity alone than can any of the other Christian virtues; and many a young soul has lived hungry for some explanation of the reason for the singularity forced upon him, quite unsatisfied by being told that the elder Friends " desired to have him encouraged." The force of example in this case has had a magnificent demonstration; but even it has failed to give the intelligent understanding of causes, without which, when the test comes, the strain must prove too great. The present crisis in the whole religious world is upon the Quaker no less than upon every other member of a sect. How many of his young people can judge, from a clear understanding of the history of their Society, whether the new problems —social, religious or moral—are counter to his own ancestors' teachings, put forth at the cost of life itself, or not? The dead bones of Quaker prophets must be made to live again in the history of their lives and all they meant, or the youth of the Society cannot be properly accounted Quakers. They will doubtless become good Christians, in the flood of modern religious teaching now surrounding them. And it is possible that this is enough, and the Quaker has done his part, and won repose. If not, then I believe that the Quakers have not sufficiently appreciated the immense chasm between seventeenth and nineteenth century needs, and that there are " crosses " far more weighty to be borne than this of the garb, which, if it be worn at all, should be regarded as a privilege. The penitential spirit of the last century Quaker, rather than combat the great evils existing in the world about him, and manfully seek to clear its political and social atmosphere, spent fruitless energy, first, in adding to the weight of this " cross " of his peculiar garb, and then in teaching his constituency how to be patient under their burden, forgetting, as Vaughan has well put it, that " there is quite as much self-will in going out of the way of a blessing to seek a misery, as in avoiding a duty for the sake of ease."

The descriptions here given have in every case had the authority of an original article of dress, or the experience of a participant in the incident quoted. Despite the lapse of time, there still exists ample material for the study of Quaker costume. Doll models still remain; the flat hat is a treasured relic in more than one family, and old silhouettes, daguerreotypes, portraits and pen drawings are to be found in many a household whose walls have never been adorned with such vanities, simply because human affection is too strong to be lightly set aside. There is no community of people among whom, as a class, family heirlooms, old plate, and the costumes of an earlier day are more highly valued or more carefully handed down from parent to child, than the Quakers. These have been called upon for their secrets of the precious past, and have been of great service in preparing the following pages, thanks to their generous owners. My acknowledgments are also especially due to Mr. Sidney Colvin, of the British Museum, for his kind permission to reproduce certain prints, and to Charles Roberts, of Philadelphia, for the use of his unique collection of Quakeriana.   A. M. G.

Haverford, Pa., 1901.

CONTENTS.

INTRODUCTION, ... iii

CHAPTER

I.—THE COAT, ... 1

II.—THE SPIRIT OF THE HAT, . . . 55

III.—BEARDS, WIGS AND BANDS, ... 91

IV.—THE QUAKERESS, ... 121

V.—THE EVOLUTION OF THE QUAKER BONNET, . . 187

ILLUSTRATIONS.

FULL-PAGE PLATES.

CHARLES I., ... *Frontispiece*
Detail from original painting by Van Dyck, in the Louvre.

OPP.
PAGE

WILLIAM PENN, ... 8
From the full-length mezzotint by Earle, of Philadelphia, after
the original painting by Inman.

"FROM LIVELY TO SEVERE," 9
I. "THE YOUTH BEFORE CONVERSION."
II. "THE YOUTH AFTER CONVERSION."

Illustrations for "War with ye Devil, or The Young Man's
Conflict with ye Powers of Darkness." 1676. By B. K.
[Benjamin Keach], Bodleian Library.

GEORGE FOX, 1624–1690, ... 26
From an engraving by Allan, after the painting by Chinn.

ELIAS HICKS, 1748–1830, ... 27
From a silhouette.

STEPHEN GRELLET, 1773–1855, ... 42
From a silhouette.

A WELSH TEA PARTY, ... 60
From a recent photograph, by courtesy of The Outlook Company.

GEORGE DILLWYN, 1738–1820, ... 61
After an engraving on stone by J. Collins.

FOUR OLD-TIME PENNSYLVANIA WORTHIES, . . 72
JOHN PEMBERTON, 1727-1795.
HENRY DRINKER, 1734-1809.
JAMES PEMBERTON, 1724-1809.
JOHN PARRISH, 1730-1807.

SEPTIMUS ROBERTS, 1807, Aged 18, . . . 73
After the etching by Rosenthal.

OPP.
PAGE

WILLIAM PENN, ... 93
After the bust in ivory by Sylvanus Bevan.

MOSES BROWN, 1738–1836, ... 106
Engraved by T. Pollock, after the portrait by W. J. Harris.

GULIELMA SPRINGETT, First Wife of William Penn, 1644-1694, 123
From an engraving after the original painting on glass, in
possession of descendants of Henry Swan, of Dorking, England.

HANNAH CALLOWHILL, Second Wife of William Penn, 1664-1726, 130
Original painting at Blackwell Hall, County Durham, England.
Copy in Independence Hall, Philadelphia.

THE COLLAR, ... 131
I. MISS FITZGERALD, LADY-IN-WAITING TO QUEEN
CAROLINE. 1800.
After the painting by Sir Thomas Lawrence.
II. MARGARET MORRIS, WIFE OF ISAAC COLLINS,
JR., 1792-1832.
From the drawing on stone of A. Newsam, after the original
painting.

"GOING TO MEETING IN 1750," 154
From an original photograph.

A QUAKER WEDDING, 1820, ... 155
After the original painting by Percy Bigland in possession of
Isaac H. Clothier, Wynnewood, Pennsylvania.

THE TWO FRIENDS, ... 164
After the engraving by Bouvier, London. About 1835.

THE FAIR QUAKER, ... 165
London, 1782.

ELIZABETH FRY, 1780–1845, ... 187
After the portrait by George Richmond, 1824.

MARTHA ROUTH, 1743–1817, ... 189
Silhouette in possession of Charles Roberts, of Philadelphia.

THE QUAKERS' MEETING, ABOUT 1648, . . . 194
After the original engraving by Egbert van Heemskerck.

OPP.
PAGE

THE CALASH, ... 206
    Invented 1765. Worn until about 1830. From an original
    photograph.

THE CAP, ... 207
    I. MARTHA WASHINGTON, SILHOUETTE.
    II. AMELIA OPIE, 1769–1853.
    Engraved by Lightfoot, from the medallion done in Paris by David.

GRACECHURCH STREET MEETING, London, 1776, . 218
    Original painting in Devonshire House collection, London.

"THE BRIDE," 219
    From the original in the "Aurora Borealis," published at New
    Castle-upon-Tyne, 1833.

QUEEN VICTORIA, ... 220
    After an engraving by Freeman. London, 1837.

FASHION PLATE, ABOUT 1849, ... 221
    From "Le Conseiller des Dames," Paris.

RAINY DAY COVER, ... 222
    From an original photograph.

ILLUSTRATIONS.

IN TEXT MATTER.

PAGE

INITIAL, MALE COSTUME, 1787, ...   3

MALE COSTUME, 1818, ...   35
    After Martin.

SUNSHADE, 1760, ...   54

INITIAL, TIME OF JAMES I., ...   57

HAT OF DOUGLAS, EARL OF MORTON, 1553,   .   .   59
    After Repton.

HAT OF CHARLES I., ...   60
    After Martin.

THE "KEVENHULLER,"   65
    After Hogarth.

OWEN JONES, COLONIAL TREASURER OF PENNSYLVANIA,   72
    Silhouette.

PURITAN HAT, ...   73

HIGH-CROWNED HAT OF 1653, ...   73

NANTUCKET BEAVER HAT, ...   75

ROYALIST HAT, TIME OF COMMONWEALTH,   .   .   90
    After Martin.

INITIAL, DR. JOHN FOTHERGILL, ...   93

PAGE

WILLIAM DILLWYN, 1805 99
Silhouette.

GABRIEL–MARC–ANTOINE DE GRELLET, 1789, . . 120
Silhouette of father of Stephen Grellet.

INITIAL, RIDING COSTUME, 1763, . . . 123
After Martin.

FEMALE COSTUME, 1835, ... 138

FEMALE COSTUME, 1787, ... 140

HEADDRESS, 1756, ... 147

LADY'S RIDING HAT, ... 156

FEMALE COSTUMES, 1776, ... 164
After Martin.

HANNAH HUNT, 1799, ... 182
Silhouette of Westtown's first scholar.

TAIL-PIECE.—SLIPPERS AND CLOGS, . . . 185

INITIAL, HEADDRESS OF REIGN OF EDWARD I., . 189

HOOD OF 1641, ... 192

BROAD-BRIMMED HAT OF ENGLISH WOMEN, 1635, . 193
From Hollar.

HEADDRESS, 1698, ... 194
From "Memoires, etc., d'Angleterre."

HOOD WORN BY CROMWELL'S WIFE, . . . 195

HEADDRESS OF CROMWELL'S TIME, ... 197
After Repton.

HOOD WORN BY CROMWELL'S MOTHER, . . 199

"LAVINIA" CHIP HAT, 1819, ... 202
Trimmed with white sarsenet ribbon.

                                                           PAGE
"CORNETTE," OCTOBER, 1816, ...   204
     Composed of tulle, quilling of blonde around face, bunch of
     flowers on top. Style is French, "simply elegant and becoming"!

HEADDRESS OF 1786, ...   209

PARISIAN PROMENADE HAT, 1816, ...   210

HEADDRESS OF 1776, ...   211
     Silhouette.

EIGHTEENTH CENTURY FLAT HAT,   .   .   .   215

BONNET OF MARTHA, WIFE OF SAMUEL ALLINSON,   .   215
     No strings, one large box-pleat in soft crown.

ENGLISH BONNET, ...   222

BONNET OF REBECCA JONES, OF PHILADELPHIA,   .   225
     From doll model dressed by "Sally Smith," of Burlington, N. J.
     Soft gathered crown, large cape with three points—one on each
     shoulder and one in center of back.

TAIL-PIECE.—BONNETS, ...   228
     "Wilburite."—1856.—"Gurneyite."

CHAPTER I.

THE COAT.

And that Friends take care to keep to Truth and plainness, in language, habit, deportment and behaviour; that the
simplicity of Truth in these things may not wear out nor be lost
in our days, nor in our posterity's; and be exemplary to their
children in each, and train them up therein; that modesty and
sobriety may be countenanced, and the fear of the Lord take
place and increase among them; and to avoid pride and
immodesty in apparel, and extravagant wigs, and all other
vain and superfluous fashions of the world; and in God's holy
fear watch against and keep out the spirit and corrupt friendship of the world; and that no fellowship may be held or had
with the unfruitful works of darkness, nor therein with the
workers thereof.   BENJAMIN BEALING, Clerk.

Epistle of London Yearly Meeting, 4th mo. 1, 1691.

CHAPTER I.

A N entire generation has passed since the distinction of plain dress, as understood by the Quakers, became obsolete in Great Britain. The singular conservatism often shown by a democratic people manifests itself in this matter, touching the social and religious life of the same body in America, by the survival in one Quaker community of the " plain " dress of a time and occasion long since gone by. The Philosopher, whose Carlylean glance comprehends the close relationship existing between man's conscience and his clothes, realizes that so far as the Society of Friends is concerned, their peculiarities of dress belong to past history. He sees also, that whether the Quakers, having accomplished a mission than which few things are more remarkable in the social and religious history of the past, are now quietly awaiting extinction, or whether they are standing in the pause for breath before they cast aside their encumbrances to plunge into the new socialism which should be their natural inheritance in the struggles of the new century,—in any case the " pride of potential martyrdom," as a recent writer puts it, has been one of the strongest elements in the old Quakerism.

In the burning moment of the first inspiration and
enthusiasm, when the watchword was, " Come out from
among them and be ye separate," the emphasis of that
separateness was sought in the minor " testimonies " of
an earnest people. Chief among those " testimonies "
was plainness of garb. But the world has counted two
centuries and a half of progress since that day, and its
myriads of Socialists, Roman Catholics, Salvation Army
soldiers, and the wide circles of a uniformed official
class, have overtaken and swept past the Quaker. His
neat garb and his honest broad-brimmed hat are no
longer conspicuous in the moderation that has followed
the periwigged days of King Charles the Second. The
Quaker has now chosen to lay aside his distinctive garb,
there being no longer the same occasion for its existence. It marks, where it still survives, the formalism
of a caste, and the day of its inspiration is over. Since
the modifications inevitable for continuance involve
the disappearance of the distinguishing outward garb of
Quakerism, it may not be amiss to seek among its
records the history of that idea of dress which, in the
early days of persecution, so strongly fortified the mar-
tyr-spirit of the Quaker. He who has the seeing eye
must know that already the beautiful garments of our
stately grandmothers, the type of Elizabeth Fry, have
gone forever. Yet let us honor the motives of high
courage and strong principle which led a whole sect to
face one of the hardest tests of the human spirit, the
world's ridicule; the sincerity of their principles is nowhere better voiced than in the " Advices " given forth
to its members by Philadelphia Yearly Meeting in
1726: " If any who may conceive the Appearance of

Plainness to be a temporal Advantage to them do put it on with unsanctified Hearts and Minds filled with Deceit. . . . Such as they are an Abomination to God and to good Men."
The *Tatler*, indeed, with its inimitable satire, shows us how clothes and religion get intermingled. It makes Pasquin of Rome write Isaac Bickerstaff:

There is one thing in which I desire you would be very particular. What I mean is an exact list of all the religions in Great Britain, as likewise the habits, which are said here to be the great points of conscience in England, whether they are made of serge or broadcloth, of silk or linen. I should be glad to see a model of the most conscientious dress amongst you, and desire you will send me a hat of each religion; and likewise, if it be not too much trouble, a cravat.*

There has been no attempt in the following pages to enlarge upon the doctrines of the Quakers. That has been sufficiently done elsewhere. The peculiarities of Quakerism " as to the outward," as Fox would have said, have been so marked, and its church polity for the past seventy-five years has been so much one of repression, that the outside world has known little of the Quaker; when it has perceived his presence, it has not troubled itself to understand him, nor to penetrate the atmosphere of exclusiveness that has surrounded him.

---

* Tatler, No. 129.—" The Old Cloak," which has been attributed to Swift, also points the same moral, although his satire is in this instance, not directed particularly against the Quakers. It begins thus :

"This cloak, it was made in old Oliver's days,
When zeal and religion were lost in a maze.
'Twas made by an elder of Lucifer's club,
Who botch'd on a shop-board and whined in a tub.
'Twas vampt out of patches, unseemly to name,
'Twas hem'd with sedition, & lin'd with the same.
This cloak to no party was yet ever true,
The inside was black, and the outside was blue ;
'Twas smooth all without and rough all within,
A shew of religion, a mantle to sin."

His dress has had much to do with this. No one has portrayed the Quaker with a worldly hand, and at the same time been just to his principles, sympathetic with his sufferings, mindful of his foibles; and it is a fact that so far no attempt has been made from within the pale to handle his garb in the light of other people's opinions and experience, to treat him just like another man, and to attempt to understand why his costume differs. The outsider has regarded the matter as little worth his time; while to the Quaker himself, the subject has been too sacred to be lightly entered upon. Its importance has been so over-emphasized, that his young people have often failed to distinguish between the doctrine of oaths and the doctrine of the coat-collar.

The present essay, then, is an attempt to trace the development of Quaker costume. It has been approached like the history of any other costume, with no detriment, we trust, to its dignity. The Quaker's interpretation of " Truth " has generally been regarded as the cause of his peculiarities in dress. And so far as the essential doctrine of simplicity as taught by Fox may go, this is eminently true. It is true, also, of some of his customs, as, for instance, the refusal to doff the hat. The following pages, however, attempt to show that the typical Quaker dress has been, in the case of the men, a survival—a crystallization, in essential elements—of the original dress of Charles the Second; while that of the women has been an evolution, having its culmination one hundred and fifty years later in the costume of Elizabeth Fry. Both have been influenced to an unappreciated degree by the fashions of a changing world; for while the Quaker walks this " vale of tears," try as he may to withdraw, he cannot part company with his fellow-citizens. His past mistake has sprung from his effort to be a " peculiar people," as well as to be " zealous of good works." Very little excites ridicule in these modern faddist days: certainly no distinctive dress of any sort. The wide philanthropy once the inheritance of Quakerism, now belongs to the world in general. Religious toleration, for which the Quakers died, bids fair to-day if not to extinguish the Society, at least to break down its hedges and boundaries. The Athenian wore his flowing robe with the wish to be plucked on the sleeve with a " what ho! Philosopher." The Quaker donned his garb from the opposite desire to be let alone. This, of course, was the Quaker position at a time when details served to emphasize the doctrines of their sect. In the two hundred and more years that have passed since the days of Fox, the occasion for such emphasis has largely disappeared. Not only among Friends, but everywhere, the different denominations are tending toward greater uniformity. This very fact makes people look leniently upon the peculiarities of the Quakers, who had the best of reasons at the time of their rise, for their various " testimonies." The anecdote may here be recalled of Penn and the King, when, to the sovereign's question wherein their religious beliefs really differed, the Quaker replied, " The difference is the same as between thy hat and mine; mine has no ornaments." The plain coat bears upon it the marks of an historical development. Warfare and politics are recorded in the cut of its collar and the sweep of its tail. Foreign influence, civil strife, diplomatic relations and political intrigue all have power to alter fashion and to impress upon a certain generation a particular style of dress. The " Steenkirk " tie, the Sedan chair, the farthingale and the " tête de mouton " are striking importations connected with foreign warfare and politics. But religious upheavals stir depths and work changes with a rapidity that nothing else can equal. Let a man's conscience once become involved in his garb, and the garb is capable of the most radical changes. The Reformation introduced simplicity at one bound into the gorgeousness of the mediæval church. Miss Hill points out that after Cranmer " it took us three hundred years to reach the simplicity of the Victorian era, while the Church accomplished the change in one generation."

There is a parallelism between clerical and Quaker garb, both in its conservatism and its simplicity of result, as well as the profound importance attached to it by its adherents. Dean Stanley tells us that the dress of the clergy had no distinct intention at the start, " symbolical, sacerdotal, sacrificial, or mystical, but originated simply in the fashion common to the whole community of the Roman empire during the first three centuries." * In the earliest times in England the tonsure was the only distinguishing mark of the clergy. Yet we all know to what elaborate proportions clerical dress had run in England by the time of Cardinal Wolsey; and the list of a few of the ordinary garments of a country parson under Henry VIII. would make an outfit sufficient for a modern theatrical show. " A gown of violet cloth, lined with red, jerkin of tawny camlet, tipped with sarcanet, two hoods of violet cloth

---

* Arthur Penrhyn Stanley, " Christian Institutions."

William Penn.

*From the full-length mezzotint by Earle, of Philadelphia,
after the original painting by Inman.*

" From Lively to Severe."

I. " The Youth before Conversion."
II. " The Youth after Conversion."

Illustrations for " War with ye Devil, or The Young Man's Conflict with ye Powers of Darkness." 1676. By B. K. [Benjamin Keach], Bodleian Library.

lined with green sarcanet, a black cloth gown trimmed with lamb."* Over against this set the reforming Cranmer, in his dark cassock and leathern girdle. As the Quaker rebelled in spirit against extravagance in dress, his impulse was not to devise a new costume, but to eliminate from that he wore, the offending elements. Hence, retaining the early cut, he evolved in the passing years a costume of his own, just as the church evolved its own distinctive dress. The clerical habit as at present worn in England dates from the time of Charles II., as did the William Penn type of dress. It is striking to note that the coat of a prominent minister among Friends in New York was given upon his death, in 1856, to a clergyman of the Episcopal Church, who wore it without requiring any change whatever! We are told that Father Greaton, the Jesuit priest who was first sent, in 1732, from Baltimore to build and settle a Romish Church in the Quaker City (which later became Saint Joseph's) was wily enough on arriving to put on the Quaker habit. He soon donned his own black clerical garb; but he was careful not to offend the Quakers in dress or speech, and his first church building might easily have been a meeting-house for plainness. The dress of the bishops of the Church of England at the present day more nearly resembles that of Penn and his colleagues than any garb of modern times; vastly more, in fact, than the " plain " dress of their spiritual descendants. This includes the linen bands, as shown in portraits of Fox and Nayler.† The clerical

* Georgiana Hill, "History of English Dress." Vol. I., p. 236.

† The original of the latter is in the library of Peter's Court Meeting-house, London.

dress-suit of the present is a correct model of the court
coat of Charles II., in cut and general style.

The most picturesque period in the whole history of
English dress was that of the princely Stuarts, as Van
Dyck has long been telling us. It was an age of swift
change and vivid contrast, of luxury and unbridled
license, when extravagance ran riot in the English
court, and wonderful tales of splendor at Versailles set
all St. James wild with envy. Great events crowded
fast upon each other; King Charles lost his royal head,
after which, for a time, the Protector and the Puritans
had things their own way. Then followed the Restora-
tion, with churchly prestige, and debauchery and extravagance striving together. A feeble attempt at
popery came next under James II., and finally an established church and prosperity under Queen Anne—all
this in the lifetime of one man! Into this scene, with
its vivid lights and its shadows unfathomable, where
Cavalier and Roundhead are eyeing each other, hand on
sword and hate in heart, steps the striking figure of the
early Quaker; and from the moment of his entrance
on the stage, a purer faith and liberty of conscience become possible in dogma-ridden England. His true part
in English history is yet to be written. Keen to de-
nounce alike luxury in the court, and crime in the
slums, loyal always to his sovereign Prince, even if refusing to doff the hat, or swear allegiance, and true
always to the impartial enlightenment of every man,
the Quaker is chiefly to be thanked for many of our
cherished religious privileges.

Could George Fox have looked ahead to this day, we
cannot doubt that he would have been perfectly satis-

fied with the simplicity of male costume in the world
at large; and that the modification must have come
without George Fox, we may be equally sure. Material
progress such as ours was not possible when men had
to guard blue satin coats and costly lace from soil.
Fancy Mr. Edison at work in lace ruffles! Even Benjamin Franklin had to roll up his sleeves. George Fox
and his contemporaries did not intend to establish a
precedent of any sort when they demanded, rather ar-
bitrarily, that their followers should discard all adornment in their dress. The Mennonites, who antedate
them by a few years, and to whom the Quakers are indebted for many of their practices, had adopted simplicity of attire as one of their cardinal principles; and
Independents, Presbyterians and others had been em-
phasizing plainness to an extreme point. The first dis-
sension in the Leyden community of Separatists came
from the lace on the sleeve of Mrs. Francis Johnson,
which furnished a subject for eleven years of strife.
Bradford says they were so rigid that some of them
were offended at the whalebone in a dress or sleeve, or
the starch in a collar. The Mennonites disapproved of
ornaments even more than the Friends did at a later
date, condemning buttons, buckles, and everything not
absolutely necessary. The Baptist Brethren in Holland (a sect that arose in Germany about 1521), were
called " Heftler " or " Knöpfler," because they excluded buttons, substituting hooks, like the Mennonite
branch in Pennsylvania, known locally as " hookers."
In some parts of the continent, rows of silver and metal
buttons were used as ornaments on coats and waistcoats; and it was chiefly against these that the Baptist

movement was directed. The use of hooks and eyes on male garb instead of buttons, was confined to such localities as had made the adornment of their clothes with a quantity of buttons an almost national custom. The plain dress of the Quakers will be found to have much more in common with the Baptists, than with the Puritans, unless we include, as is often erroneously done, most of the dissenting sects of England under the latter head. In the United States, certainly, the many Puritan laws as to the dress of both sexes, and the elaborate detail of rules regarding every minor item, with the frequent enumeration of costly and extravagant fashions, lead us inevitably to the conclusion that the New England Puritan was far from the plain and meek person our fancy has been taught to draw; but rather that he was gorgeous in his highly colored raiment, his wigs and velvet; that his wife was a positively appalling person in her finery, so soon as prosperity had come to the thrifty pair in their adopted land.

We can respect the feelings of the first Quakers as to ornaments, for their " testimony " had a distinct object to accomplish; many felt with Ellwood about " those Fruits and Effects of Pride, that discover themselves in the Vanity and Superfluity of Apparell which I, so far as my Ability would extend to, took alas! too much delight in. This evil of my doings I was required to put away and cease from; and Judgment lay upon me till I did so. Wherefore, . . . I took off from my apparel those unnecessary Trimmings of Lace and Ribbands and useless Buttons which had no real service, but were set only for that which was by Mistake called Ornament, and I ceased to wear Rings." *

---

* Journal of Thomas Ellwood.

By a very similar line of spiritual experience, Thomas Story was led to a point where the vanity of human wishes was forcibly presented to him; for even before learning of the peculiar tenets of the Friends, he had adopted some of their outward characteristics, in discarding sword and ornaments of dress. He did not meet the man whose influence led him to become a Quaker until 1691; yet in 1689, to use his own words:

I put off my usual Airs, my jovial Actions and Address, and laid aside my Sword, which I had wore, not thro' design of Injury, or Fear of any, but as a modish and manly Ornament. I burnt also my Instruments of Musick, and divested myself of the superfluous Parts of my Apparel, retaining only that which was necessary or deem'd decent. The Lust of the Flesh, the Lust of the Eye and the Pride of Life, had their Objects and Subjects presented; The Airs of Youth were many and potent; Strength, Activity and Comeliness of person were not a-wanting, and had their share; nor were natural Endowments of Mind or Competent Acquirements afar off, and the Glory, Advancements and Preferments of the World, spread as Nets in my View, and the Friendship thereof beginning to address me with flattering Courtship. I wore a sword, which I well understood, and had foil'd several Masters of that Science, in the North and at London; and rode with firearms also, of which I knew the Use; and yet I was not quarrelsome; for though I emulated, I was not envious; But this rule I formed as a Man to myself, never to offend or affront any wilfully, or with Design; and if, inadvertently, I should happen to disoblige any, rather to acknowledge, than to maintain or vindicate a wrong thing; and rather to take ill Behaviour from others by the best Handle, than be offended where no offence was wilfully designed. But then I was determined to resent, and punish an Affront or personal Injury, when it was done in Contempt or with Design; and yet I never met with any, save once; and then I kept to my own Maxims with Success; and yet so as neither to wound nor be wounded; the good Providence of Almighty being ever over me; and on my side, as ever knowing my Meaning in all my Conduct.*

---

*Thomas Story, Journal, Folio ed., p. 15.

The Quakers, in fact, will be found to have held a
middle ground between the austerities of the old-line
Cromwellian Puritans and Roundheads, and the extravagances of the Cavaliers. The peculiarities to
which in later days they so closely adhered, were the
outgrowth natural to a body which clung to practices
that were once established, with the tenacity of larger
but no less strongly organized religious bodies, like the
Roman Catholics, the Mohammedans, or even the
Chinese. A distinctive form of dress was at no time
adopted by the Quakers with " malice prepense." The
fact that in the second century of their existence a
peculiar garb came to be regarded as so essential, goes
to prove, not vitality, but rather a period of decadence
in their religious principles. The marked changes that
Quaker costume has undergone, while they have not
kept pace with the outside world as regards frequency
of modification, are yet important as an element in
studying the history of the sect. A cause is often
greatly strengthened by the moral support of a distinctive and conspicuous style of dress, as for instance,
that of the Salvation Army. John Wesley regretted
that he had not made a regulation about dress. He
wrote in his Journal: " I might have been firm (and
I now see it would have been far better) as either the
people called Quakers or the Moravians; I might have
said, this is our manner of dress, which we know is both
scriptural and rational. If you join with us, you are
to dress as we do, but you need not join us unless you
please; but, alas! the time is now past."

George Fox, however, did not dream of such measures among his own people. The simple, unadorned

costume of the men of his generation was all that Fox
aspired to. Along with his admonitions as to all ways of
living, he included in his denunciations every extravagance of dress. This alone meant a revolution difficult
for us to realize. The extremest form of Paris fashion
to-day would be simplicity itself compared with the
dress of an English aristocrat in the time of the first
Charles. Until the early part of the eighteenth century, there appears to have been no really distinctive
cut in Quaker costume. It is to be described in nega-
tions, was like that of every one else, and was only conspicuous for what it lacked of the popular extravagances
of the day. When men wore even more elaborate costumes than women, as in the days of the " merry monarch," anything plain was noted at once. Cromwell's
dress was so much more simple than that of the kings
before and after him, that Quaker simplicity was in his
time less conspicuous. The Protector was very frugal
in attire. He wore black cloth or velvet, sword-scarf,
trunk-hose, long boots, grey hat and silver clasp; varied
at times with doublet, cloak and hose of coarse cloth
turned up with velvet, and stockings of grey worsted
reaching over the knee to meet the hose. His hair
was simply arranged, without curls, and was somewhat
long behind. His moustache was so small as to be
quite inconspicuous. At fifty-eight he looks like a
Quaker himself, with his muslin collar and long hair.
In his portrait, by Walker, in the National Gallery, a
page ties his sash. Quakers and Puritans under the
Protector were more distinguished for differences of
opinion than differences of garb. An old author declares that " short cloaks, short hair, short bands and

long visages " were the rule. What we understand as the typical Quaker garb, worn by William Penn, was a survival of that of Charles the Second, when the distinctive outward marks of Quakerism were burned into the sect, so to speak, by the rigors of persecution. The dress of Fox was more nearly that of Charles the First. This was to be expected of the plain countryman, who would naturally cling to the more old-fashioned garb; he never discarded the doublet, and always wore his own hair long; whereas Penn, the diplomat and courtier, followed the fashions in the cut and style of his dress, adopting the full-skirted coat of the sovereign, and wearing as many as four wigs in one year.

To test the correctness of this comparison, let us take the costume of Charles the First as we have him in the great portrait by Van Dyck in the Louvre. The King wears a hunting dress consisting of white satin coat, knee breeches in red, long boots with square toes, flat lace collar, long hair, a pearl drop in the left ear (which he even wore to his execution), and carries an enormously long cane. Divest him now of all his superfluities. Remove the enormous feather in his hat, and Fox's own broadbrim stands revealed. Both King and subject wear the hair " banged " on the forehead, falling in long locks on the shoulder—only the curls and perfume are wanting in the Quaker. The lace worn by the King at throat and wrists is missing altogether with Fox, plain bands only being visible over his drab coat, which buttons to the throat, and takes the place of the King's satin doublet and rich cloak. But every other man of plain origin wears a doublet of similar cut to that of Fox, the drab in his case being for the sake of economy, and hence simplicity in not dyeing the cloth. Leathern breeches and jerkins were universal among the " plainer sort," as George Fox called them, and were also worn from motives of economy. Trousers were not to be invented for another century. The style of knee-breeches, stockings and low shoes is identical with Fox and his King. The only difference is one of ornament. Fox's breeches have no " points," as the elaborate bows of jewelled ribbon at the knee were called; the stockings are of homespun, not silk, like the King's; and the heavy, square-toed shoes are minus the elaborate ribbons on the instep. Even the long cane is common to both. Samuel Smith, of Philadelphia, who kept a Journal, and who died in 1817, aged eighty-one, says of his travels in England: "At Samuel Lythall's, where we lodged, I saw the staff, it is said, George Fox used to travel with—a large cane stick about four feet in length and ivory head—looked as though it might have belonged to a country squire, and probably had been Judge Fell's." *And this is all.* The dress of the Quaker, when he first arose, was in cut and fashion simply the dress of everybody, with all extravagances left off; and since costume was then so elaborate, his perfect simplicity was quite enough to draw attention and render him conspicuous, even had he held his peace.

> O transmutation!
> Of satin changed to kersey hose I sing.*

But this he could not do, and many were his testimonies. In 1654, Fox wrote:

---

*Newcut, in "The City Match," I, 4. By Jasper Mayne, 1639.

My spirit was greatly burthened to see the pride that was got up in the nation, even among professors; in the sense whereof I was moved to give forth a paper directed

" TO SUCH AS FOLLOW THE WORLD'S FASHIONS.

"What a world is this! how doth the devil garnish himself! how obedient are people to do his will and mind! They are altogether carried away with fooleries and vanities, both men and women. They have lost the hidden man of the heart, the meek and quiet spirit; which with the Lord is of great price. They have lost the adorning of Sarah; they are putting on gold and gay apparel, women plaiting the hair, men and women powdering it; making their backs look like bags of meal. . . . They must be in the fashion of the world, else they are not in esteem; nay, they shall not be respected, if they have not gold or silver upon their backs, or if the hair be not powdered. But if one have store of ribands hanging about his waist at his knees, and in his hat, of divers colours, red white black or yellow, and his hair powdered, then he is a brave man, then he is accepted, then he is no Quaker. He hath ribands on his back, belly, and knees, and his hair powdered: this is the array of the world. . . . Likewise, the women having their gold, their patches on their faces, noses, cheeks, foreheads, their rings on their fingers, wearing gold, their cuffs double under and above, like a butcher with his white sleeves; their ribands tied about their hands, and three or four gold laces about their cloaths; this is no Quaker, say they. . . . Are not these, that have got ribands hanging about their arms, hands, back, waists, knees, hats, like fiddler's boys? And further, if one get a pair of breeches like a coat, and hang them about with points and up almost to the middle, a pair of double cuffs upon his hands, and a feather in his cap, here's a gentleman; bow before him, put off your hats, get a company of fiddlers, a set of music, and women to dance. . . . They are not in the adorning of the Lord, which is a meek and quiet spirit, and is with the Lord of great price."

Late in life, in Second month, 1690, he issued from the home of his stepson-in-law, William Meade, at Gooseyes, whither he had retired in feeble and broken health, a note of warning directed " To such as follow the fashions of the world."

Thomas Ellwood, whose Journal is one of the most graphic pictures of the day, but who, it is to be hoped, was a better tutor than poet, thus bewailed the prevalent extravagance:

But Oh! the Luxury and great Excess
Which by this wanton Age is us'd in Dress!
What Pains do Men & Women take, alas!
To make themselves for arrant Bedlam's pass!
The Fool's py'd Coat, which all wise Men detest,
Is grown a Garment now in great Request.
More Colours now in one Waist-Coat they wear
Than in the Rainbow ever did appear.

. . . .

And he that in a modest Garb is drest,
Is made the Laughing-stock of all the rest.
Nor are they with their Baubles satisfy'd,
But sex-distinctions too are laid aside;
The Women wear the Trowsies and the Vest,
While Men in Muffs, Fans, Petticoats are drest.

He warns Friends of the danger of the modes, and says:

It hath come to pass that there is scarce a new Fashion come up, or a fantastick Cut invented, but some one or other that professes Truth, is ready with the foremost to run into it. . . . Assuredly, Friends, if Truth be kept to, none will need to learn of the World what to wear, what to put on, how to shape or fashion their Garments, but Truth will teach all how best to answer the end of clothing. . . . Let every one examine himself that this Achan, with his Babylonish Garment, may be found out and cast out, for indeed, he is a Troubler of Israel.*

"Babylonish garments" sorely troubled the Friends, and it was with those of them who were tailors by trade much as it was with John Mulliner and

*Thomas Ellwood, Journal, p. 343.

his musical instruments.* Gilbert Latey, a very interesting character of that early day, was a master tailor,
whose attention to business, combined with his natural
tact and uprightness, had won for him a very lucrative
trade among the worldly, so that he was patronized by
the gentlemen of fortune about the court. Becoming
one of the " Children of the Light," he was no longer
able to make the gay clothing that the fops of the day
required, and he imperilled his fortune by declining to
take any more such orders, although eventually a
steady plain trade remained to him as his reward of
faithfulness. King Charles the Second, while out
hunting one day, met him upon the road, and the merry
monarch called out to the Quaker tailor to step up to
his horse's side for a chat, after which, with words of
cheer, the King rode to his hounds, while the Quaker
pursued his way to meeting.†

But the question of dress became more and more important as the cessation of active persecution gave the
Friends time to devote more attention to its details.
Dress was every day growing more and more extravagant; there seemed no limit to the extremes which it
might reach. A cursory glance at the old fashion
plates of this period, or an examination of Hogarth's
works of a satirical character, will show us in a moment the reason for the emphasis laid on dress by the
early Quakers—not the earliest, however, for these had
been occupied with a struggle that involved life itself,
and had no time for attention to clothes. Between

---

* See chapter on Wigs.
† Beck and Ball, " History of London Friends' Meetings," p. 250.

1660 and 1680, men's dress underwent many more changes than that of women. A large portion of a gentleman's time was given over to his elaborate toilette, and fortunes were squandered on lace and wigs by the fops and ladies of fashion. To these evils the Quakers very naturally directed their condemnation, and the subject became a prominent one in the care and instruction of their youth. How to guard a young man from the dangerous fascinations of a periwig that measured some three or four feet in length, or a young woman from a spreading farthingale, or a tight bodice in which she could barely draw the breath of life, may not seem to us now so very difficult; but we may be assured that the struggle was a hard one. No matter into what eccentricity Dame Fashion led her followers, they were willing to be guided by any blind extravagance; and the youthful Quaker cast longing eyes in her direction, even if she masqueraded in wig or farthingale, petticoat-breeches or wide hoop. More and more stringent became the laws of the Quakers on the subject; and while Aberdeen seems to have breathed in the atmosphere of the Scotch Covenanters a spirit more rigid than is to be found anywhere else in the limits of the Society, London and Dublin were not far behind. It is instructive to notice that drab tape was just as bad as red tape.

In 1686 the Meeting in Dublin seems to have shown very high order of talent in dealing with the question of dress, and went to the root of the matter when it attempted to purify the source of supply. The General Meeting appointed meetings of tailors " to see that none did exceed the bounds of truth in making of ap-

parel according to the vain and changeable fashions of
the world ; " and these meetings of " merchant tailors and clothiers " reported to the church. They very
judiciously advised Friends to " wear plain stuffs and
to sell plain things, and tailors to make clothes plain."
And also to ensure their wishes, " Friends would do
well to employ Friends that are tailors, for the en-
couragement of those Friends of that trade that cannot
answer the world's fashions." This may be the reason, as Barclay * suggests, that Dublin Friends were
spared the details of Christian simplicity that appear
on the books of their Scotch brethren, and from which
we may get an insight into the drastic measures of
Aberdeen and Edinburgh. The trade plan, we are told,
worked so well, that in 1693 they invoked the aid of
joiners, ship-carpenters, brass-founders, saddlers and
shoe-makers, to give their judgment to the meeting " in
the matter of the furniture of houses, etc., etc."; " fine,
shining, glittering tables, stands, chests of drawers and
dressing-boxes; " " large looking-glasses and painting
of rooms," as well as " painted or printed hangings."
Where these latter were needful, they would do well to
advise with concerned Elders of their meetings before
they put them up.

The Overseers of the church traveled over the country. They inspected the shops to see if " needless
things were sold," such as " lace and ribbons." They
inspected the houses with ornamental " eaves," and of
superfluous size, from the drawing-room curtains, with
other " Babylonish adornings " which were declared to

---

* Robert Barclay, " Inner Life of the Religious Societies of the Commonwealth."

be " needless," to the kitchens whose array of " shining, needless " pewter and brass pots, pans and candlesticks were evidently for ornament, and therefore contrary to the " simplicity of truth." Figured, striped or flowered stuffs, cloths or silks were, about 1693, generally condemned. As Barclay, from whom we have already quoted, says: " The whole life of man, from the cradle to the grave, was legislated upon; the ornaments on his cradle were to be dispensed with. Mothers were to suckle their children. It hath also been recommended to our Women's Meeting causing [concerning?] their child-bed dressings and superfluities of that nature that things may answer the plainness of Truth's principles both in themselves and their children from their births upwards. Coffins ought to be made plain, without covering of cloth or needless plates." In 1717 they order that chaises, except when absolutely necessary, are a needless luxury. The food, dress and even the gait of the children come under the care of the officers of the meeting, as well as the deportment of the nursemaids! In 1719 " floor-cloth," or the new fashion of carpets, was denounced, grateful to the feet of young and old on the cold, chilly floors in an English winter, but savoring of other vanities then being introduced with the growth of the Eastern trade under the care of the new East India Company. The question was, how far can one go before a comfort becomes a snare or a vanity. A vast amount of time was wasted in searching for the line of demarcation. Just before this, " the fashionable using of tea " (another Eastern importation, now become as national as the Union Jack), was ordered to be avoided; tea-tables to be laid aside, " as formerly advised "; and snuff, snuff-boxes, and the chewing and smoking of tobacco, " *except when needful*," are reprobated! Tobacco, in the early days, was more universally used among the plain Friends than now. William Penn is said to have enjoyed his pipe, as did many another worthy. An unlocated minute of Ninth month, 1691, runs:

It being discovered that the common excess of smoaking tobacco is inconsistent with our Holy Profession, this meeting adviseth that such as have occation to make use of it, *take it privately*, neither in their Labour nor employment nor by the highway, nor alehouses or elsewhere, too publicly.*

The climax, however, is reached, when we are told that a lowly mind would rather " admire the wonderful hand of Providence " in contemplating the necessary than the beautiful in nature, and the eye is not to be indulged in " great superfluity and too great nicety in gardens." In other words, turnips and cabbages tend to keep the mind humble, but the rose and the lily may prove a snare! And this, in the land of gardening and wall-fruit, where even the gooseberry is idealized! It surely is a wonder that all artistic sense has not been crushed out of the sect in two hundred years of such arbitrary dictation to the consciences of people, as may be found through the greater part of the eighteenth century among the Quakers, when they were a prosperous, not a persecuted, body. But the elasticity of human nature, and the eternal demand for some outlet to his pent-up artistic enthusiasm, is being manifested to-day in the reaction of the modern young Quaker in favor of music and the arts generally.

* Manuscript copy of old English Minutes, in possession of the author, made by Henry Hull, of New York, 1850.

The plain Quaker administered a silent reproof to all extravagance wherever he appeared, and the lampoons and broadsides of the day began their scurrilous attacks almost as soon as church and state combined to persecute him in earnest. One reason that we have heard so little of the anti-Quaker literature of 1655 to 1700 is because of its indecency. At a time when nobody was nice in speech or manners, it can hardly be imagined to what depths the popular lampoon sank; so that we are forced to leave these bits of Quaker history where we find them—buried in musty collections in the public libraries of England, or on the shelves of American antiquarians. It is necessary, however, to note their existence, since they show how the world regarded the Quaker. Those quoted are among the most decent. The Quakers were derided and pursued by every one. Their simplicity was said to be for purposes of deception; their frugality and consequent thrift were mocked at as penuriousness; their marriages without the priest were declared illegal, and their children were scoffed at as illegitimate. No stone was left unturned to render their lives a burden. This was a popular description:

A Quaker is an everlasting Argument; For like Afrique, he is daily teeming with some new Wonder; he that can describe him fully may boast he hath squared the circle. . . . His looks and habit cry "Pray observe me", and his whole deportment is starched and affected; you may take his face for a new-fashioned Sun-Dyal, where the forced wrinkles represent Hower lines, and his Tunable nose the gnomen. If he wants money, he need only say to one of his gang "The Lord hath sent me to borrow of thee 40 shillings." . . . These new seers ramble about to establish certain little Fopperies, as if the Salvation of the World depended on the Preaching down of Points, Cuffs, Tyth-Pigs and Pulpit-Hour-glasses; he is a kind of spiritual Gypsy that describes Grace and Piety by the Lines of the Physiognomy, and

confines Christianity to such a Complexion or habit, being con-
fident that cannot be a wedding garment that hath any trimming. . . . But 'tis no small attempt to encounter a Party whose
Impious PENN hath presumed to duel the sacred Trinity.

> " A candle of himself can't stand upright;—
> The reason is, because his head is light." *

An anti-Quaker tract of 1679 † says: " The Quakers
cry out against all external ornaments, whilst them-
selves at the same time doat most wickedly upon a
Quirp-cravat, copied from a Chitterling original."
The Quaker was universally known as " Aminadab."
Says Misson:

> The Quakers are great Fanaticks; there seems to be some-
> thing laudable in their outward Appearance—they are mild, sim-
> ple in all respects, sober, modest, peaceable—nay, and they have
> the reputation of being honest; and they often are so. But
> you must have a Care of being Bit by this Appearance, which
> very often is only outward.‡

Such universal dislike was the logical result of their
contrast to the exaggerated verbiage and ornate dress
of the time. It is natural to expect less difference between the early Quakers and the " world's people " in
cut and style of dress than in the society even seventy-
five years after the death of Fox, for the very good

---

* " Plus Ultra, Or the Second Part of the Character of a Quaker,
etc." 1672.

† " Work for a Cooper. Being an answer to a Libel." 1679.
Printed by J. C. for S. C. Prince of Wales Arms.

‡ " Les Quacres sont de grands fanatiques. Il parvit en eux quelque
chose de louable : il semble qu'il soient doux, simples à tous égards, sobres,
modestes, paisables: ils ont même la réputation d'être fidèles, et cela est
souvent vrai. Mais il ne faut pas s'y tromper, car il y a souvent aussi bien
du fard dans tout cet extérieur."

" Memoires et Observations faites par un Voyageur en Angleterre,
1698." Quoted by Repton, in an article On the Development of Hats
and Bonnets, from the Time of Henry VIII., to the Present Day.
Published in Archæologia, Vol. XXIV., p. 174.

George Fox, 1624-1690.

From an engraving by Allan, after the painting by Chinn.

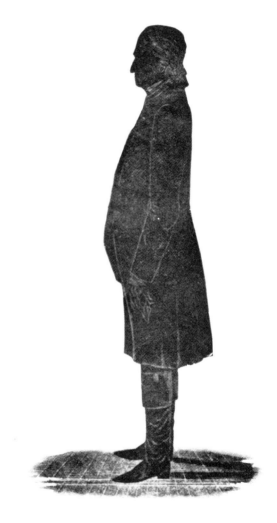

Elias Hicks, 1748-1830.

From a silhouette.

reason that when persecution was following them, and
they were being scourged, imprisoned and beaten to
death, dress was a subject little dwelt upon. Simplicity
only was taught; no distinctiveness other than that induced by its practice. A few years later matters are
very different,* and the cut of the coat has become
almost an essential in the plan of salvation. The process
of adoption of a Quaker fashion has thus been described
by an anonymous English writer † :

> A novelty in dress is at first regarded as objectionable; then
> it is admitted and not considered inconsistent; and lastly, when
> the rest of men have passed from it, it is clung to with all the
> devotion which our society entertains for its peculiar customs.
> Where are now the cocked hats that were at first a vanity and
> afterward the outward visible signs of Quakerism, and have now
> . . . disappeared? Where are the green aprons that became us
> as a people? Where is the testimony against trousers, that, if
> one may trust tradition, once agitated the Society, and was the
> theme of discourses that claimed to be the utterances of eternal
> wisdom?

Our author concludes by saying that if we wear to-
day George Fox's coat, we cannot retain the principle;
if we retain the principle, we cannot retain the coat.
" A Pious Gentleman that had been thirteen years
among the Separatists to make observations," wrote
warningly in a Broadside to his countrymen in 1657:

---

* William Penn, Jr., to James Logan :

" Worminghurst, Aug. 18, 1702.
" My dress is all they can complain of, and that but decently genteel,
without extravagance; and as for the poking iron (sword), I never had
courage enough to wear one by my side."
Howard M. Jenkins, " The Family of William Penn," p. 109.

Soon after, his father, the Founder, thus writes of him to James
Logan in Pennsylvania : " Pray Friends to bear all they can, and melt
toward him at least civilly, if not religiously." Ibid., p. 111.

† " Nehushtan ; A Letter addressed to the Members of the Society of
Friends on their Peculiarities of Dress and Language." London, 1859.

The Puritan Spirit was the spirit of Quakerism in the first degree,—which thing wise men know full well. . . . For 1 know, countrymen, what I say, that three parts of you that are religiously affected at this day are possessed with that humour that will make you Quakers if you take not great heed.*

Banbury was a great stronghold of dissenters, chiefly Presbyterians; but many Quakers were yearly tried at the Banbury Assizes, from the neighborhood of Oxfordshire. Castor, in " The Ordinary," an old play by Cartwright, 1651, says:

> I'll build a cathedral next in Banbury;
> Give organs to each parish in the Kingdom,
> And so root out the unmusical sect.†

The cant of the Presbyterians laid them open to an equal amount of ridicule with the Quakers. Little Wit in " Bartholomew Fair," is made to say: " Our mother is a most elect hypocrite, and has maintained us all this seven year like gentlefolks."

An old play, " The City Match," makes Aurelia thus remonstrate against the preaching tendencies of her Presbyterian maid:

> " Oh, Mr. Banswright, are you come? My woman
> Was in her preaching fit; She only wanted
> A table's end."
> Banswright.   " Why, what's the matter ? "
> Aurelia.   " Never
> Poor lady had so much unbred holiness
> About her person: I am never drest
> Without a sermon: but am forced to prove
> The lawfulness of curling-irons before
> She'll crisp me in the morning. I must show
> Text for the fashions of my gowns. She'll ask
> Where jewels are commanded? Or what lady
> I'th primitive times, wore ropes of pearl or rubies?

* " Anti-Quakerism, or The Character of the Quaker Spirit." London, 1659.
† Act II., Sc. 3.

> She will urge councils for her little ruffs
> Call'd in Northamptonshire, and her whole service
> Is but a confutation of my clothes.*

The long grace of the Presbyterian was another of his characteristics often ridiculed. We read of

> One that cools a feast
> With his long grace, and sooner eats a capon
> Than blesses it.

or this:

> Dost thou ever think to bring thy ears or stomach to the patience of a dry grace as long as thy tablecloth; and droned out by thy son here till all the meat on thy board has forgot it was that day in the kitchen, or to brook the noise made in a question of predestination by the good laborers and painful eaters assembled together, put to them by the matron, your spouse, who moderates with a cup of wine ever and anon, and a sentence out of Knox between? †

The Quakers were thus derided in a similar way:

> Water us young Shrubs, with the Dew of Thy blessing; that we may grow up into Tall Oaks, and may live to be saw'd out into Deal Boards, to wainscot Thy New Jerusalem! ‡

The Puritans, as we have seen, emphasized plainness of garb, but evaded the spirit of the law when they wrought embroidered texts upon their garments with a view to " moralize " them. The old play, previously quoted, has the following:

> Nay, Sir, she is a Puritan at her needle, too:
> She works religious petticoats; for flowers
> She'll make church histories; besides,
> My smock-sleeves have such holy embroideries,
> And are so learned, that I fear in time
> All my apparel will be quoted by

---

* Jasper Mayne, " The City Match." 1639.

† " Quarlous," in " Bartholomew Fair," Act I., Sc. 1.

‡ " The Quaker's Grace." Thomas Brown, " Works, Serious and Comical." London, 1720.

Some pure instructor. Yesterday I went
To see a lady that has a parrot; my woman,
While I was in discourse, converted the fowl;
And now it can speak but Knox's Works;—
So there's a parrot lost.*

The Puritan ladies showed great ingenuity in the choice and execution of some of the sacred themes that appeared upon the garments of members of their families. The custom lived but a short life, because of its elaborate and expensive development. The texts and sacred scenes that were thus worked upon clothing in lace and embroidery, remind us of the fourteenth century fashion of emblazoning armorial bearings upon the dress. This custom became general in France during the reign of Charles V. A general sumptuary law in the time of the Roses, applied to all classes, forbade cutting the edges of sleeves or borders of gowns into the form of letters or other devices; and the tailor who made such gown was subject to imprisonment.† The extravagant display of gold lace and thread grew among the Puritans to an abuse that rapidly put an end to this sort of " moralizing," which was in every way opposed to the professed simplicity of Puritanism. We read in Beaumont and Fletcher:

Having a mistress, sure you should not be
Without a neat historical shirt? ‡

The range of color in Quaker clothing seems to have been early limited to the browns and grays. Thomas Ellwood says that there was a man in the Monthly Meeting at Isaac Pennington's who " had his eye often

---

* Jasper Mayne, "The City Match." 1639.
† Georgiana Hill, "History of English Dress." Vol. I., p. 137.
‡ "Custom of the Country." Act II., Sc. 1.

upon me, for I was a young Man and had at that time
a black Suit on." This was, of course, very early in the
period of Ellwood's convincement. The women had a
rather wider scope at first, but after the opening of the
eighteenth century plain colors were universal among
the Quakers. In the neighborhood of Oxford, indeed,
brown was under a ban for a short time. "Heretofore
Friends chose to wear grey clothing out of a dislike to
brown, because it bore the name of a certain man of
Abingdon that had stuck close upon the skirts of
Friends thereabouts." * All wearing apparel was
treated seriously, and was bequeathed to relatives and
friends, and great minuteness was shown in disposing
of it. The laborer in Queen Anne's day wore the broad
brim, flat, felt hat that had been discarded by the man
of fashion; a jerkin or short coat, knee breeches and
heavy yarn stockings. The breeches were often of
leather, adding to the neutral coloring in the matter of
dress. The man of the world, on the other hand, was
correspondingly gay. Even Robespierre, a century
later, as Carlyle tells us, wore a sky blue coat, a white
silk waistcoat, embroidered with silver, black silk
breeches, white stockings, and gold shoe buckles. The
doublet in Charles the Second's time was cut; it then
became longer than before, and was adorned with the
new buttons, just introduced, down the front. There
was one royal attempt at reformation in dress, but it
did not succeed.†

---

* See "Quaker's Art of Courtship," by the author of "Teague-
Land Jests—Calculated for the Meridian of the Bull and Mouth." Abingdon had long been famous for its woolens, even then.

† For the new costume of the King, see Pepys' Diary, Vol. VI.,
p. 29. "A long cassock close to the body, of black cloth pinked with
white silke under it, and a coat over it, and the legs ruffled with black
riband like a pigeon's leg." Oct. 15, 1666.

By the end of this reign the picturesque old doublet had vanished and the King's coat was almost of the eighteenth century cut. The dragoons of this and the succeeding reign wore their brilliant red coats in the new square fashion, with ample sleeves, and skirts turned back with two buttons. This was the coat worn by everybody for the next hundred years, Quakers as well as others, with slight modifications. It was not until the end of the century that coats became short and grew a tail. William Penn's skirts were full—and why? Because the Stuart reign demanded a sword under the coat—quite as a mere matter of decency; and when William renounced the sword it did not strike him as at all necessary to curtail his ample skirts in anticipation of what, one hundred years later, came to be known as the " shad-belly " of his Pennsylvania successor. Yet skirts could be too full, even then.

20th. of 9 mo. 1688. It is concluded that the Friends appointed in every particular meeting shall give notice publicly in the meeting that cross-pockets before men's coats, side slopes, broad hems on cravats, and overfull skirted coats are not allowed by Friends.*

The American Friends were not behind their English cousins in this matter of plainness, and earlier even than this period had been warning their constituency of the dangers of conformity to worldliness.

In 1695 Philadelphia Yearly Meeting advised:

That all that profess the Truth and their Children, whether young or grown up, keep to Plainess in Apparel as becomes the Truth and that none wear long-lapped Sleeves, or Coats gathered at the Sides, or Superfluous Buttons, or broad Ribbons about their Hats, or long curled Periwiggs, and that no Women, their Children or Servants dress their heads immodestly or wear their

---

* MS. of Henry Hull.

Garments indecently as is too common; nor wear long Scarves; and that all be careful about making, buying or wearing (as much as they can) strip'd or flower'd Stuffs, or other useless & superfluous Things, and in order Thereunto, that all Taylors professing Truth be dealt with and advised Accordingly.

Also advised, "That all Superfluity & Excess in Buildings and Furniture be avoided for time to come." Change had to come among the Quakers, however, as it had in the world. By the middle of the eighteenth century the country folk were following more closely in the wake of the town. "Fifty years ago," says a writer in 1761, "the dress of people in distant counties was no more like those in town than Turkish or Chinese. But now in the course of a tour you will not meet with a high crowned hat, or a pair of red stockings." Miss Hill goes on to say:

The high crowned hat was pretty well confined to the Quakers, who were as noticeable for the neatness as for the old-fashioned cut of their garments. Their linen was always fine and clean, and the quality of their sober colored coats and gowns was of the best. The most rigid discarded all additions which could in any be described as ornaments, even to the buttons with which it was the fashion to loop up the hats. The men's hats were lower and wider brimmed than the women's, which were of the regular steeple shape. Quakers, of course, did not wear wigs.*

Upon the matter of wigs we must correct Miss Hill. Many Quakers wore them, including William Penn.

In August, 1787, the London "Chronicle" published a satirical paragraph of advice to a man of fashion relative to correct costume for seaside wear:

For the morning, provide yourself with a very large round hat. This will preserve your face from the sun and wind, both of which are very prejudicial to the complexion. Let your hair

---

* Hill, "History of English Dress." Vol. II., p. 167.

be well filled with pomatum, powder and bear's grease, and tuck it under your hat.　Have an enormous chitterling* to your shirt, the broader the better, and pull it up to look as like the pouter pigeon as you possibly can.　A white waistcoat without skirts, and a coat with a collar up to your ears will do for an early hour; and if they say your head looks like that of John the Baptist on a charger, tell them you are not ashamed to look like an Apostle, what ever they are!　Your first appearance must be in red morocco slippers with yellow heels; your second in shoes with the Vandyke tie; your third in Cordovan boots, with very long rowelled spurs, which are very useful to walk in; for if you tear a lady's apron, it gives you a good opportunity of showing how gracefully you can ask pardon.　Your fourth dress must be the three cornered hat, the Paris pump, and the Artois buckle.†

The foregoing is valuable as showing how far dress had become modern in 1787.

Red heels were worn under Louis XIV., and in the time of Louis XV. these were made of wood in bright red at Court, and were considered a great mark of gentility.‡　Shoe buckles adorn the shoes of Louis XIV. in his portrait by Rigaud in the Louvre, painted in 1701; they came into England in the reign of William III., and by the end of the eighteenth century were enormous.　Then came the French Revolution, which affected even shoe buckles, and they were supplanted by ribbons or strings.　The American Quaker sea-captain, John M. Whitall, who visited England in 1819, relates that he wanted to go to meeting in Liverpool, and had a struggle in mind over putting leather strings in his shoes, instead of the worldly ribbons he would have had to buy.　But he did not "gratify pride" to that extent!§

* A ruffled front, falling from the neck.
† Hill, " History of English Dress." Vol. II., p. 128.
‡ Quicherat, " Histoire de Costume en France," p. 562.
§ Hannah W. Smith, " Diary of John M. Whitall," p. 107.

Men in 1786 carried enormous muffs. These had a
ribbon attached to suspend them from the neck, with a
bow of ribbon tied in the center. The beau went about
encumbered with this, a sword and a very long cane, no
doubt with the *"very jantee"* air that the old books
refer to as the *sine quâ non* of the modish gentleman of
two hundred years ago. Muffs had come to America
as early as 1638. Dr. Thomas Prence, in Boston, in
1725, lost his "black bear-skin muff"; and several
muffs were left by will in New York in 1783.* An old
French print shows a " Quaquer d' Amsterdam " in the
dress of William Penn, carrying an enormous muff.
Buttons of great size adorned everything possible under Charles the Second, and paint and " patches " prevailed. The riding-coats of this period were red, but in
1786 we find them green, with enor-
mous mother-of-pearl buttons. It was
about this time that a Frenchman in
Philadelphia wrote that on a certain
day in September the Quakers in that
town " put on worsted stockings to a
man ! " †

1818.
(After Martin.)

In the first years of the nineteenth
century the worldly coat took on the
cut-away effect seen in portraits of
Jeffersonian times; and here we have
the origin of the modern " plain coat,"
which is in reality a nondescript affair,
being, as to its collar, a survival of
the coat of Penn, who, however,

---

*Alice Morse Earle, " Costume of Colonial Days," p. 164.
† Elizabeth Drinker, Journal.

would have been horrified at its height; and as to its tail, an early nineteenth century mode. Something in its shape appealed to an American wag long ago, who, struck by its resemblance to the fish familiar to our shores, dubbed it the " shad ! " Had it been possible, the Quakers would doubtless still have clung to the early style of dress, but their bravest efforts were of no avail. The coat of William Penn had no collar whatever, as we have seen. There came a time when the worldly coat rose straight up to a line behind the ears, and the neckcloth passed in many folds about the choked and gasping neck, tilting the chin, for air and ease, to a point which carried the nose upward and gave the beaux of the period a most supercilious air. The familiar portrait of Robespierre will illustrate this, when all the gentlemen of England were aping the fashions of the Directoire. Presently, because it could rise no higher, the worldly coat-collar dropped over in a roll, and the neck was released from all its swaddling bands of cambric. The Quaker stopped at this point; he had followed the fashion a quarter of a century behind, it is true, but still followed, his coat collar creeping up by imperceptible degrees until the middle of the nineteenth century. At the present time only a faithful few are left to struggle against the inevitable roll, and these few are in America, Friends in the mother country having ceased to observe an obsolete convention. It took the coat collar a full two hundred years to rise to its greatest height and fall in the snare of a worldly roll—what more natural than that the Quaker collar should be as long in rolling?

Seventy-five years ago trousers were among the

things viewed by conservative Quakers with very grave
suspicion. The evolution of the "pantalon," its rise,
name, origin and effect are described by Quicherat.*
The garment seems to have come from Venice in the
sixteenth century. The Venetians were called "Pan-
taloni" in upper Italy, and the Italian comedians introduced the garment in France, in fantasy and ballets.
The court of Louis XIII. danced "en pantalon," as did
Richelieu himself, for the edification of Anne of Austria. The breeches were first lengthened to the calf,
meeting the reversed boot-top, but trousers did not become popular at that time for stout wear, because the
supreme hour had not yet come in which to discard the
boot. Without attempting to dwell on the history of
the most modern garment worn, it may be as well to remind ourselves that trunk hose had just been succeeded
in Fox's time by breeches to the knee, adorned with
fringe and ribbon; "petticoat breeches," frilled and
voluminous, having been a short-lived mode. What
George Fox would have done with trunk hose it would
be interesting to know! At their height a law was
necessary forbidding a man to carry "bags stuffed in
his sacks"—a mild form of smuggling. A person before a court justice, when charged by the judges with
being habited contrary to the statute, convinced them
that the stuffing was not composed of any prohibited
article, inasmuch as it "contained merely a pair of
sheets, two tablecloths, ten napkins, four shirts, a brush,
a comb and a nightcap !" †

By the end of the eighteenth century there was a
growing plainness in men's dress, and Charles James

---

* Quicherat, " Histoire de Costume en France," p. 480.
† "The Book of Costume. By a Lady of Quality." London, 1846.

Fox and his friends in the House of Commons aided its coming. 13 May, 1807, one Hamilton, at Balliol College, Oxford, wrote: " No boots are allowed to be worn here, or trousers or pantaloons. In the morning we wear white stockings, and before dinner, regularly dress in silk stockings," etc. In 1808 the " trousered beau " was present. He had before this worn silk stockings, velvet knee breeches, powdered wig, cocked hat and sword.* All through the eighteenth century Quakers wore knee breeches, with silk or yarn stockings, according to their circumstances in life, and low shoes or riding boots. It is interesting to learn from Miss Hill that knit stockings were only worn some fifty years before Fox was born. They had before been of cloth or continuous with the clothing, as in the days of trunk hose. Pepys' stockings were of silk and wool. When the " pantalon " arrived from Italy, the first were of plain light cloth, fitting very tightly. By 1830 they were much as they have since remained, the " cossack " shape being the transition, reminding us of Dr. Holmes' lines:

> They have a certain dignity that frequently appals,
> Those mediæval gentlemen, in semi-lunar smalls.

" French Pantaloons " are advertised in a Philadelphia newspaper of 1828.

In 1798 Mrs. Lloyd wrote to her son Robert, who had gone up to London to visit his friend Charles Lamb:

> I was grieved to hear of thy appearing in those fantastical trousers in London. I am clear such eccentricities of dress would only make thee laughed at by the world, whilst thy sincere friends would be deeply hurt. . . . Neither thy mind nor person are formed for eccentricities of dress or conduct.†

---

* Hill, " History of English Dress." Vol. II., p. 233.
† E. V. Lucas, " Charles Lamb and the Lloyds," p. 97.

Robert Lloyd, in 1809, wrote to his wife:

Pray dispatch me from the Dog Inn at seven o'clock in the evening, 2 pair of White Silk stockings. I must go smart to the Opera. I have ordered a pair of dress-clothes in London.

His brother Charles inquires of him about the same time:

If Hessian boots would do to wear with pantaloons or small clothes indiscriminately, I should prefer them, but not without.*

The Lloyds were of Quaker stock, and a charmingly cultivated family, to whom the friendship of Charles Lamb was sure testimony of wit and culture. They did not remain in the circle of Quakers, but intermarried with the Wordsworths, and from them sprang three Bishops and an Archbishop of the Established Church! The English Quakers, however, were not alone in their dread of the new fashion.

When Mr. Jefferson discarded his short breeches, silk stockings and low shoes with silver buckles, and concealed his well-formed legs in pantaloons, the Federalists were prone to regard it as the trick of a demagogue to secure favor with the mob. A gentleman in trousers and short hair! But what better could be thought or expected of a Democrat and an atheist?

In 1867, folks forty years old could remember the high stock, cruel shirt collar, ruthless coat-collar, the prodigious bonnet and general severity of costume before Channing, Dickens, Beecher, and the New York "Tribune" had begun to emancipate the American understanding from its tight fitting armor of opinion.†

Mrs. Earle tells us that the colonists of Massachusetts Bay landed, some in doublet and hose, and some in coat and breeches. The fact is interesting to the student of Quaker dress, for it is another evidence that there must have been great variety of costume among the

* Ibid., p. 268.
† James Parton, " The Clothes Mania."

different classes of society in England in the seventeenth century. The first mention of trousers in this country was in 1776, although they are possibly the "tongs" or "tushes" of 1638. The garment was at first put to the use of what we now call overalls. The Pilgrim men wore buff breeches, red waistcoats, and green or sad-colored "mandillions." * The indignant Stubbes was also moved to inveigh against "mandillions" in a passage that gives a perfect picture of the coat and jerkins of the late sixteenth and early seventeenth centuries. He says:

Their coates and ierkis, as they be diuers in colours, so be they diuers in fashions; for some be made with collors, some without, some close to the body, some loose, which they cal mandilians, couering the whole body down to the thigh, like bags or sacks, that were drawne ouer them, hiding the dimensions and lineaments of the body; some are buttoned down the breast, some vnder the arme, and some down the backe, some with flaps ouer the brest, some without; some with great sleeues, some with small, some with none at all; some pleated and crested behinde and curiously gathered, some not; and how many dayes (I might saye houres or minutes of houres in the yeare) so many sortes of apparell some one man will haue, and thinketh it good prouision in fayre weather to lay vp agaynst a storme.†

Doublet and hose were worn more in the Southern colonies than in New England, and were richer in material. In the list of "apparel for 100 men," of the Massachusetts Bay Company, Mrs. Earle tells us that doublet and hose may be found in 1628, but they had disappeared in New England by 1635. The doublet was worn in England also by women in 1666, to the

* "'Mandillions,' a sort of doublet, fastened with hooks and eyes, and lined with cotton."—Alice Morse Earle, "Costume of Colonial Times," p. 218.
† Philip Stubbes, "Anatomie of Abuses." Ed. 1586, p. 49.

scandal of our friend, Mr. Pepys. As has been noted, George Fox wore the doublet all his life. What was known as " hair camlet " seems to have been a fashionable material among the plainer Friends for coats, while the gayer, or, as the phrase went, " the finer sort," wore velvet of various colors. John Smith, of Burlington, New Jersey, going to " pass meeting " for the first time previous to his marriage with Hannah, the daughter of James Logan, of Pennsylvania, 28th of Eighth month, 1748, wrote in his diary, " I put on a new suit of hair camlet." *

The dress of Jonathan Kirkbride, of Pennsylvania, born in 1739, is thus described by a descendant, and the description may be taken as that of many Quakers of the middle of the last century. Its cut is much like that of Elias Hicks.

During his preaching expeditions, he went out mounted on a pacing horse, a pair of leather saddle-bags, containing his wardrobe, hung behind the saddle, a silk oil-cloth cover for his hat, and an oilcloth cape over the shoulders, which came down nearly to the saddle, as a protection from storms. Stout corduroy overalls, with rows of buttons down the outside to close them on, protected the breeches and stockings. A light walking stick did double duty, as a cane when on foot, and a riding whip when mounted. . . .

He wore a black beaver hat, with a broad brim turned up at the sides so as to form a point in front and rolled up behind; a drab coat, with broad skirts reaching to the knee, with a low standing collar; a collarless waistcoat, bound at the neck, reaching beyond the hips, with broad pockets, and pocket flaps over them; a white cravat served for a collar; breeches with an opening a few inches above and below the knee, closed with a row of buttons and a silver buckle at the bottom; ample silver buckles to fasten the shoes with; fine yarn stockings. . . .

In winter, shoes gave place to high boots, reaching to the knee in front, and cut lower behind to accommodate the limb.

---

* " The Burlington Smiths," by R. Morris Smith, p. 153.

When he adopted pantaloons, with great reluctance, just before his death, at an advanced age, he complained of their feeling " so ' *slawny*,' flapping about the ankles ! " *

The men Friends of the early nineteenth century wore for an overcoat a long collarless garment of heavy cloth, like Gay's

> True Witney broadcloth, with its shag unshorn,

which was usually known among them as a " surtout," worldly French name though it was!

> That garment best the winter's rage defends
> Whose ample form without one plait depends;
> By various names, in various countries known
> Yet held in all the true surtout alone.
> Be thine of kersey firm, though small the cost;
> Then brave unwet the rain, unchill'd the frost.†

Possibly none clung to knee breeches longer than some of the Quakers in America, and the last instance that I have found is that of Richard Mott, who for forty years was clerk of New York Yearly Meeting, and who died in 1856. His daughter-in-law writes, in a letter preserved among old family papers:

> Mother Mott is better again. She is making [him] a pair of pantaloons, and I am helping her. The men have nearly all got to wearing them now, and he looks and feels so singular in his " smalls," that he could not stand it any longer, but bought some beautiful cloth in New York for the purpose.‡

Sometimes it is not clear what particular point in the costume was criticized, as at Dartmouth, Massachusetts, whose Records say:

---

* Mahlon S. Kirkbride, " Domestic Portraiture of our Ancestors Kirkbride; 1650–1824."

† Gay, " Trivia."

‡ Hannah B. Mott to her mother, Hannah Smith, from Mamaroneck, N. Y., 8 mo. 23, 1828.

27th. 1 mo. 1722; 'The visitors give account that they have been with B. S. who is gone from ye order of Friends into ye fashion of ye world in his apparel, who signified that he is resolved to have his own way.

Benjamin, we learn, was disowned; but the minutes are silent as to what he wore, which we should very much like to know. A rather more serious case was that of C. G., Jr., who on the 15th of Third month, 1756, " made an attempt to lay his intentions of marriage before the Preparative Meeting at Acoaxet & was not admitted by reason of his wearing fashionable clothes." He was labored with by the Friends, but refused to change his worldly apparel, married " out of the order," and was eventually disowned.

At Nantucket, Massachusetts, 1801, L—— H—— was disowned for " deviating from our principles in dress and address." We find that he persisted in wearing buckles, and refused to use " thee " and " thou." In 1803, at the same meeting, it is recorded that H—— C—— " had deviated in dress and address from the plainness of our Profession." *

The inventory of the household goods and clothing of Benjamin Lay, the extraordinary Anti-Slavery Quaker of Pennsylvania, is still in existence; and this curious and unique account is sufficiently instructive to warrant its partial reproduction. It will be noted that the list includes " britches " and trousers, the former of leather in several cases,† as well as a " skin coat," and jacket of the same leather as the " britches." Various cloaks and riding hoods, and seven or eight other

---

* Worth, " Nantucket Friends' Meetings."

† William Strypers in 1685, had " two pair of leather breeches, two leather doublets, handkerchiefs, stockings, and a new hat." This constituted the outfit of the Dutchman, when he settled in Germantown, Pa., at that date. " Settlement of Germantown," by Judge Pennypacker, p. 128.

hoods in white or black, had evidently belonged to his wife, whose death took place some years before that of her husband, in 1742. Sarah Lay was also a little hunchback, an English woman, and an acknowledged minister in the Society of Friends, who accompanied her husband when he first came to America in 1731. She evidently had not been ensnared by so worldly a fashion as the bonnet, which was far from the thoughts of the good Quakeress of that date. The few items that follow are selected from the original manuscript with an eye to the style of garments worn by the Lays. Benjamin Lay died Second month 3d, 1759, aged 82. The sale (or "vendue," as the document reads) occurred the next month, and fills fifteen folio pages of description. £68 17s. 1d. were realized. The list includes one hundred and twenty-five books, mostly Friends', a copy of Plutarch's Lives, etc. His home was near Abington, Pa. The last rather startling item in this list evidently refers to a piece of damaged goods!

INVENTORY OF CLOTHING
OF
BENJAMIN LAY, OF PENNSYLVANIA,
DIED 2 MO. 3RD. 1759.

	s	d
Coat and Jacket	2	6
Buckrim Coat	0	4
2 Jackets and a frok	1	2
Plush coat	9	7
Pare of Leather Britches	3	11
Leather Jacket	5	0
" "	4	1
"	1	8
Skin Coat	0	3
Pare of Shoos	6	6
Coat and Hat	1	1
Bag and pare of Cloth boots	2	5

	s	d
Leather Jacot	10	3
Coat .	1	6
Pare of Britches	11	6
" "	4	0
Trunk .	2	0
Cloke .	1	6
A Hide and cloke	1	6
2 flanell petty cote	3	3
Clock [cloak] and riding-hood	2	4
Petecoat .	3	1
Crap gound [crêpe gown]	3	1
Calleminco gound	4	6
Camblit "	1	1
Quilted petecoat	10	1
Winder curtins	1	11
Black silk scarf 1	18	0
Ditto . 1	17	1
Black silk scarf 0	18	0
Black hood	11	0
Whit silk "	3	9
A " " "	5	0
Ditto .	4	1
A silk handkerchief	7	0
Ditto .	2	9
A silk handkerchief	7	0
pare of silk gloves	5	0
" " gloves .	1	10
A whit hood	2	3
" linen "	1	4
Ditto .	2	0
2 muslin handkerchiefs	4	1
A whit hood	3	1
" "	4	1
3 " aprons	5	11
Pocket handkerchief	5	1
6 caps	4	9
" "	4	8
10 "	5	3
3 cambric handkerchiefs	4	4
8 pinners	7	0
A checkard apron	2	3

		s	d
20 neck cloths		4	3
sundry mittens		2	3
a green apron		2	0
Ditto		2	4
a pare of pockets		1	0
3 pare worsted stocks		4	7
1 dimity wastecoat & 2 shifts		18	0
12 diaper napkins & 2 table-cloths	3	10	0

Besides shirts, stockings, gloves, " 17 shifts," 12 table-cloths, towels, napkins, sheets, pillow-cases, " curtins," " a hammack," quilts, " vallians," etc., " to numerous to mention."

Also, a variety of dry-goods in the piece, 40 lbs. whalebone, thimbles, needles, buttons, 12,000 pins, stay-tape, 1 doz. flints; and finally, " 8 yards of damnified ozonbriggs! "*

The dress of Nicholas Biddle is described by the Frenchman, M. de Bacourt, so late as 1840, as " a blue coat with brass buttons, yellow nankeen pantaloons, canary colored gloves, and a glossy beaver." The same M. de Bacourt is said to have made the *mot*, that the " world is ruled by three boxes—the ballot-box, the cartridge-box, and the band-box! "

The only title of honor recognized by Friends seems to have been that of Doctor. The ills of the flesh were so heavy in the days before the use of modern methods of healing, that the physician who could in any way alleviate suffering was made welcome for his kindly services, and his title was generally given him. England was far behind Holland in the healing art, and Friends went to the Netherlands, where Leyden was famous in science and learning, to study medicine. A flourishing body of Quakers already existed in Amsterdam. Anatomy and physiology were taught with

---

*Ozonbrigg—One of the many materials with Eastern or other curious names, so much in use in the sixteenth and seventeenth centuries. Spelt also Oznaburg, Ozenbridge, etc. ; originally made at Osnabrück, Hanover. Linen. (Alice Morse Earle.)

Dutch thoroughness, and Rembrandt's great painting, " The Anatomist," was a correct representation of the scientific training which that nation was giving to the whole world. The Doctor, in the seventeenth century, was a great social personage. His power and his presence were only second to that of a great church dignitary. No one ever questioned his authority on any point, and to his utterances the people paid great heed. He had but just stepped over that mysterious borderland lying between mystery and science, and to the unlettered of his day, his knowledge was hardly to be attained without supernatural means. Both on the continent and in England he wore a distinctive dress. The black cloth garb was quite clerical in effect, and the great bush wig was invariably accompanied by a gold-headed cane. Portraits of Doctors Fothergill and Lettsom, both very eminent men, and both Quakers, show them in clothing of rather lighter hue, but with the adjuncts of cocked hat, wig and cane. The Quaker profession in England maintained the courtesy and the garb without, however, any of its exaggerations; and respect for their calling led them to wear the wig throughout the period of its history—a motive which did them honor, although, at this date, we may not be able to recognize any added sentiment of beauty or dignity in that adornment.

In America, democratic as it was—and yet most conservative, so far as adhering to a style of dress is concerned—the wig was not considered *de rigueur* among Friends, where its adoption, with Doctors, as with other mortals, was entirely a matter of taste. We can therefore the better understand Ann Warder's aston-

ishment at the appearance of a Doctor in Philadelphia,
wearing none of the insignia of his profession. She
writes, in 1786, " We dined at Nicholas Waln's in company with there sisters and two public Friends." (A
usual term for minister among the Quakers.) " One,
I understood, was a country Physician, but how would
he look by the side of ours, instead of a great Bush
Wig, and everything answerable, his Dress was as humble as possible." At meeting, the next day: " The
Doctor I mentioned yesterday appeared beautifully ";
that is, he preached or prayed acceptably to his audience. The Doctor of Divinity also shared in a professional costume as he does now, and this lends meaning to the note of Thomas Story, who in 1717, at Rad-
nor, Pennsylvania, in describing meetings he had held
at that place, says: " We heard also of a Doctor of
Divinity in one of our meetings, disguised in a blue
coat; but not of any objections made." *

The new thing, whatever it might be, was viewed
askance by Quakerism, which, in America, at least, was
never more fearful of innovations than during the
period immediately succeeding the departure of the
Quakers from the Pennsylvania Assembly in 1756.
They withdrew from active life, and paid more attention to the limitations of dress and custom among their
membership, and this grew upon them with the passing
years. Richard Talbot, of Ohio, was visited by Friends
of his Yearly Meeting for putting on *suspenders;* and
umbrellas caused many anxious moments when they
were introduced among the Friends. The first umbrella carried in Edinburgh was borne by Alexander

---

* Thomas Story, Journal, p. 573. (Folio.)

Wood, a surgeon, in 1782. It was a huge gingham apparatus, clumsy and awkward to a degree. It was also a surgeon who the following year carried a yellow glazed linen umbrella down Glasgow streets, justly proud of the new importation from Paris. Before this, huge green paper fans were employed as a protection from the sun, while the rainy-day devices were many. Jonas Hanway, however, although he has the credit of carrying the first umbrella in London, in 1756, must now give way to a Philadelphia Quaker, for on February 20, 1738, an "umberella" was imported to Philadelphia in the good ship "Constantine," as shown by the invoice, for the "proper account and risque" of Edward Shippen, who, indeed, for aught we know, may have worn out that nine shilling umbrella long before Jonas Hanway carried his.* Nathaniel Newlin carried the first umbrella to Chester (Pa.) Meeting, and to this evidence of a worldly spirit Friends took great exception, and made remonstrance, although Nathaniel was a person of weight, and had sat six times in the Pennsylvania Assembly.

As for the women, they had long been used to following the advice of Gay:

Good housewives all the winter's rage despise,
Defended by the riding hood's disguise;

but it was considered a very feminine and unmanly performance at first to be seen carrying an umbrella, and only women might

Underneath the umbrella's oily shed,
Safe through the wet on clinking patten tread.
Let Persian dames the umbrella's ribs display,
To guard their beauties from the sunny ray;

* " Pennsylvania Magazine of History and Biography." Jan., 1901.

Or sweating slaves support the shady load,
When Eastern monarchs show their state abroad.
Britain in winter only knows its aid,
To guard from chilling showers the walking maid.*

The grandmother of the Philadelphia lady who vouches for the following had a no less thrilling experience in the attempt to be in the mode than had Nathaniel Newlin. During her girlhood her father brought her an umbrella. She carried the novel gift with great pleasure and delight, but so new and unknown was the article that the meeting to which she belonged became alarmed and the Overseers dealt with the worldly-minded father. During the controversy one woman Friend said to the young girl, " Miriam, would thee want that held over thee when thee was a-dyin' ? " That of course settled the matter, and the offending umbrella was relegated to seclusion. Many present necessities of the toilet were unknown luxuries in the early days. We are told that in 1650 Sir Ralph Verney sent to a friend a present of " teeth-brushes and boxes," which were new-fangled Parisian articles, called by him, " inconsiderable toyes." †

There are few more sensitive souls than that of sweet and tender John Woolman, to read whom in these sordid days is like a breath from the Elysian Fields. We could not all find it possible, or even our duty, to live so near his ideal; for to few human beings is it given to so completely sever their connection with the world, and the things of the world. Nevertheless, there is no more salutary reading for these strenuous days than the small but precious contribution made by John

---

* " Trivia."
† Georgiana Hill, " Women in English Life." Vol. I., p. 158.

Woolman to the body of English literature. He is here
named because of the travail of soul that he endured
over his clothes; for to him, poor dear, the dye in his
garments was as great an object of uneasiness of spirit
as the lack of it would have been to William Penn! He
tells us in his Journal, that amazing record of a soul's
experience, that " the thought of wearing hats and garments dyed with a dye hurtful to them, had made a lasting impression on me." This was in the year 1760,
when the Quaker tailor was just forty years old, and his
calling had led him to see the vanities of men rather
intimately.

This, and the wearing more clothes in summer than are needful, grew weary to me, believing them to be customs which have
not their foundation in pure wisdom. The apprehension of being
singular from my beloved friends was a strait upon me; and thus
I continued in the use of some things contrary to my judgment.

But our Journalist fell ill and in the depths he records his mind brought into a state of perfect submis-
sion to the will of God, as he interpreted it. For nine
months he continued to wear out the garments he had
already in use, and then his first move in the direction
of the new reform was to buy an undyed hat.

I thought of getting a hat the natural color of the fur, but
the apprehension of being looked upon as one affecting singularity felt uneasy to me. Here I had occasion to consider that
things, though small in themselves, being clearly enjoined by Divine authority, become great things to us; and I trusted that the
Lord would support me in the trials that might attend singularity, so long as singularity was only for His sake. On this account I was under close exercise of mind in the time of our General Spring Meeting, 1762, greatly desiring to be rightly directed;
when, being deeply bowed in spirit before the Lord, I was made
willing to submit to what I apprehended was required of me,
and when I returned home got a hat the natural color of the fur.

No portrait, alas, exists of John Woolman, but this lets us know that his hat was a beaver of the natural color. Doubtless he would never have consented to have his "counterfeit presentment" taken. He had some mental stress because of this step, for he adds that after this,

In attending meetings, this singularity was a trial to me, and more especially at this time, as white hats were used by some who were fond of following the changeable modes of dress, and as some Friends who knew not from what motives I wore it grew shy of me, I felt my way for a time shut up in the exercise of the ministry. . . . My heart was often tender in meetings, and I felt an inward consolation which to me was very precious under these difficulties. Some Friends were afraid that my wearing such a hat savored of an affected singularity; those who spoke with me in a friendly way, I generally informed, in a few words, that I believed my wearing it was not in my own will. I had at times been sensible that a superficial friendship had been dangerous to me; and many Friends being now uneasy with me, I had an inclination to acquaint some with the manner of my being led into these things; yet upon a deeper thought I was for a time most easy to omit it, believing the present dispensation was profitable, and trusting that if I kept my place, the Lord in His own time would open the hearts of Friends toward me. I have since had cause to admire His goodness and loving kindness in leading about and instructing me, and in opening and enlarging my heart in some of our meetings.

Surely nothing could be more beautiful than the spirit here shown, although a practical mind might find some criticisms possible. But if all the Friends to-day bought their hats and bonnets in the same spirit, it would surely not be long before the Society of Friends again became a power in the world. Shall any one hereafter say that there is nothing of philosophy in clothes? The Quaker custom of self-examination and comparison with the ideal life, and a disparagement of native gifts

and talent, made the humility in which the Quaker was
" clothed as with a garment," and which he seldom
ceased in the last century to recommend, take on sometimes a melancholy hue.

Aggressive as the Quaker garb would seem to have
been upon a superficial glance at the situation, it will be
found that the sect made no effort to force their peculiarities upon the public, nor have they ever done so.
They and their hats became conspicuous by force of circumstances, and of course were at once in the public
eye. They did not preach Quaker, but only plain
dressing; and they would at first have denied their public position on the subject had they been given the
choice. The Quakers have always had the good sense
to hold quite in the background their views on dress,
when they have gone out as missionaries to what we are
pleased to call " the heathen." And herein they have
been wise in their generation. How much good would
they have accomplished, for instance, by insisting that
a Hindu woman should at once put on the plain bonnet? It is quite as reasonable to expect the Quakers to
adopt the Chinese dress, as, indeed, more than one has
done. There is a beauty of line in certain forms that
Quaker dress has taken, that is pleasing to the artist,
and possesses still more attraction for the moralist or
historian. It is hardly perceptible to him who is unfamiliar with Quaker history. The modern idea of
beauty in dress is no longer one of personal adornment,
but there is a moral quality that enters into it, which is
quite the product of the last three hundred years. The
merely decorative element is one that has always appealed to the savage on the plains, or in Central Africa.

The purely æsthetic side of dress was present to the Greek as never before or since; and to the Knight in armor came a sense of protection together with the appeal to his prowess. But it is only of late years that we have had a conscience in our clothes; and what is beautiful must now stimulate our feeling for the best and truest. We do not object to the peculiarities of the Quaker garb as did the public in Oliver Cromwell's day, to whom it was offensive because an implied reproach. But we see in it the memory of martyr and saint and hero, and we suffer it, because to us it stands as a symbol of some of the qualities for which the human soul has greatest need. A feeling of sadness creeps over our mind that its history has become altogether that of the past.

Sunshade. 1760.

Stephen Grellet, 1773-1855.

From a silhouette.

CHAPTER II.

THE SPIRIT OF THE HAT.

Any Cappe, whate'er it be,
Is still the signe of some Degre.
"Ballad of the Caps," 1656.

Ne dit-on pas qu'il ne faut pas penser avoir toutes ses
aises en ce monde?
Lois de la Galanterie.

CHAPTER II.

TWO hats in the history of the church stand forth conspicuous from the mass. In shape they are not unlike. The oldest has a round crown, and plain wide brim, and is unadorned save for cord and tassel. Gorgeous in brilliant red, it typifies churchly prestige and power; and the cardinal who wears it is a functionary of what has been the most powerful church organization on the face of the earth. To but one other hat has ever attached so much religious significance. That is the drab broadbrim of the early Quaker. How many controversies have been waged, how many hard words flung over the apparently simple matter of the hat! On this futile subject we have had countless tracts, pamphlets and sermons; while lawsuits, loss of property and loss of life are all on record. The spiritual welfare of an entire sect has at one time seemed to depend on the manner of wearing the covering for the head. The whole "testimony" of the early Quaker against the frivolities of his day was concentrated in his hat.

It is important to remember that the period was but just past when this had been a part of the costume, no more to be removed when entering the house or seated at table than the shoes or doublet. Hats were worn in church, and the clergy preached in them. The elegant courtiers at the French and English courts were now beginning to greet the ladies and their superiors in rank with the new sweeping bow—"making a leg," as it was termed—with consummate grace and art, the hat's long, graceful feather sweeping the floor in the action.

This is not a Parisian fashion book, nor yet a history of worldly costume; nevertheless, we must seek the origin of the Quaker hat among the abodes of fashion. This part of the costume has a very interesting history, and might in itself fill a good-sized volume. The felt hat with which we are chiefly concerned goes back to the time of the early Greeks. There is a felt hat on a statue of Endymion in the British Museum. The Normans at the conquest wore hats of the same durable material, and we love the "flaundrish bever hat" of the Merchant, in the Canterbury Tales. Among the peasantry of the seventeenth century, the old English and Scotch "bonnets" were worn, usually of cloth or other heavy stuff, low and broad in shape; while at all times in the early history of England some variety of the hood was to be found among both sexes alike. Chaucer's Reve was rewarded by his master with "thanks, a cote and hood"; and the Monk—

"For to fasten his hood under his chinne,
He had of gold ywrought, a curious pinne."

At the coronation of Anne Boleyn, the Aldermen "toke their hoddes from their necks, and cast them about their shoulders." * The old time-honored bonnet had been superseded by the hat in the early sixteenth century; and in the reign of Henry VIII., we find certain old prints that give us the jaunty hat always asso-

* Archæologia, Vol. XXIV., p. 172.

ciated with that monarch, showing the hood still worn underneath it, or thrown over the shoulder. Felt hats had been found most durable for soldiers' wear, and their lasting qualities made them popular with the common people. Ashton tells us that a new-fashioned beaver hat, sometimes called felt and made by the Dutch, came in about 1559. They were afterward made in England by the Dutch refugees at Wandsworth, and were a luxury only to be afforded by fine gentlemen. A good hat was very expensive, and important enough to be left among bequests in a will. They were borrowed and hired for many years, and even down to the time of Queen Anne, we find the rent of a *subscription hat* to be two pounds six shillings per annum! There must have been great peace and harmony in the wearing of that hat, one would think! In the time of Elizabeth beaver hats were an extravagant luxury, and " were fetched from beyond the seas, where a great sort of other varieties do come beside." The hats were small at first, and one old writer says:

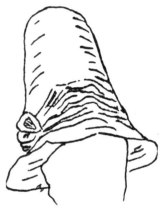

Douglas, Earl of Morton.
1553.
(After Repton.)

"So propre cappes,
So lytle hattes,
And so false hartes
Saw y never." *

The " hattes " soon grew as broad as that of the Wife of Bath, and were known as " castors." The print of a

---

* " Maner of the World Now-a-Days."

fashionable man of 1652 has the hat-brim extending horizontally, with a long drooping feather, threatening

to fall. This was the hat of Charles the First, which has since come down to us as the Quaker broad-brim. The steeple - crowned hat of James I. still exists in

Hat of Charles I.
(After Martin.)

beaver in Wales, worn by both men and women, the latter placing it over the hood or cap in the manner of the first Quaker women. Nothing has ever destroyed the hold of the felt hat upon the affections of the English nation.

> " The Turk in linen wraps his head,
> The Persian his in lawn too;
> The Russ with sables furs his cap,
> And change will not be drawn to;
> The Spaniard's constant to his block,
> The French inconstant ever;
> But of all felts that can be felt,
> Give me your English beaver." *

Old Philip Stubbes, in 1585, wrote of

HATS OF SUNDRIE FATIONS.†

Sometymes they vse them sharpe on the croune, pearking vp like the spere, or shaft of a steeple, standyng a quarter of a yarde aboue the crowne of their heades, some more, some lesse, as please the phantasies of their inconstant mindes. Other-some be flat and broad on the crowne, like the battlemetes of a house. An other sorte haue rounde crownes, sometymes with one kinde of band, sometymes with another, now blacke, now white, nowe russed, now redde, now grene, nowe yellowe, now this, now that, neuer content with one colour or fashion two daies to an ende. And thus in vanitie they spend the Lorde his treasure, consuming their golden yeres and siluer daies in wick-ednesse and sinne. And as the fashions bee rare and strange,

---

* " English Mutability in Dress."
† Philip Stubbes, " Anatomie of Abuses," 1586.

A Welsh Tea Party.

From a recent photograph, by courtesy of The Outlook Company.

George Dillwyn, *1738-1820.*

After an engraving on stone by J. Collins.

so is the stuffe whereof their hattes be made diuers also; for some are of silke, some of ueluet, some of taffatie, some of sarcenet, some of wooll, and, whiche is more curious, some of a certaine kinde of fine haire; these they call beuer hattes, of xx. xxx. or xl. shillinges price, fetched from beyonde the seas, from whence a greate sorte of other vanities doe come besides. And so common a thing it is, that euery seruyng man, countrieman, and other, euen all indefferently, dooe weare of these hattes. For he is of no account or estimation amongst men if he haue not a ueluet or taffatie hatte, and that must be pincked, and cunnyngly carued of the beste fashion. And good profitable hattes be these, for the longer you weare them the fewer holes they haue. Besides this, of late there is a new fashion of wearyng their hattes sprong vp amongst them, which they father vpon a Frenchman, namely, to weare them with bandes, but how vnsemely (I will not saie how assie) a fashion that is let the wise judge; notwithstanding, howeuer it be, if it please them, it shall not displease me.

And another sort (as phantasticall as the rest) are content with no kinde of hat without a greate bunche of feathers of diuers and sondrie colours, peakyng on top of their heades, not vnlike (I dare not saie) cockescombes, but as sternes of pride, and ensignes of vanity. And yet, notwithstanding these flutterying sailes, and feathered flagges of defiaunce of vertue (for so they be) are so advanced in Ailgna [England], that euery child hath them in his hat or cap: many get good liuing by dying and selling of them, and not a few prove theselues more than fooles in wearyng of them.

Bright, in " Bartholomew Fair " (Ac⁺ .., Sc. 4), says:
By this two-handed beaver, which is so thin
And light, a butterfly's wings put to 't would make it
A Mercury's flying hat, and soar aloft.

And Edgeworth, in the same play:
See him steal pears in exchange for his beaver hat and his cloak, thus.

Gay afterward wrote:
The Broker here his spacious beaver wears;
Upon his brow sit jealousies and cares.*

---

* " Trivia."

A list of clothing for Prince Henry, eldest son of James I., in a bill rendered by Alexander Wilson, tailor, September 28, 1607, contains "a side hunting coat camblett wrought alle thicke with silke galowne in 2 together [double ?] with a whoode [hood] of same camblett," etc. Also, "Beavers of divers colours, lined with satin or taffeta," at sixty shillings each, and "new dying and lining three beavers with taffeta or sateen," five shillings.* Plumes on the broad hat came in at the end of the sixteenth century, and continued to the time of Queen Anne. The Spanish Dons on the streets of London were familiar figures in their flat-crowned hats and short cloaks, taking snuff prodigiously and smelling of garlic. Plain broad-brim hats of shovel shape were worn a good deal in the country and by poorer Londoners for many years after this, when the cocked hat had begun its long and eventful reign. Samuel Pepys, to whose invaluable diary we must often turn, tells us, under date of November 30, 1663: "Put on my new beaver"; and the next year he says: "Caught cold by flinging off my hat at dinner." In a note to this passage in Lord Clarendon's "Essay on Decay of Respect due to Old Age," the author says that in his younger days he never kept his hat on before his elders "except at dinner"! This custom lasted into the next century. Pepys says again (February 22, 1666-7): "All of us to Sir W. Pen's house, where some other company. It is instead of a wedding dinner for his daughter. . . . We had favors given us all, and we put them in our hats, I against my will, but that my Lord [Brouncker] and the rest did." This was doubt-

---

* Archæologia. Vol. XXIV. 1793.

less at table. Planché says that the absence of hats in the print of the banquet for Charles II. can only be accounted for by the presence of the sovereign. The gentleman of fashion in 1695 wore his hair long under a broad plumed hat. The jeweled sword at his side dangled from an embroidered scarf; enormous coat cuffs concealed his hands, when they were not thrust into a huge muff. The large bordered hat was turned up at three sides, and until 1710 kept the adornment of plumes. After that the cord and ribbon seem to have been adopted.* These flapping brims grew so broad as to necessitate looping up, and hence the origin of the cocked hat, which had a long and honored career. The absence of cocking denoted the sloven.†

"Take out your snuff-box, cock, and look smart, hah," says Carlos, in Cibber's "Love makes a Man." Their numerous shapes are alluded to by Budgell ‡: "I observed afterwards that the variety of Cock in which he moulded his Hat, had not a little contributed to his Impositions upon me." That man was to be guarded against "who had a sly look in his eye, and wore the button of his hat in front." Both sexes wore small looking-glasses. Men even wore them in their hats. In

---

* " Le bas de milan, le castor,
   Orné d'un riche cordon d'or."
   —Quicherat, " Histoire de Costume en France," p. 474.
An early poem, " The Mercer," belonging to the thirteenth century, (Percy Soc., Vol. XXVII., p. 9,) says : " J'ai beax laz à chapeax de feutre." ("I have beautiful lace for beaver hats "). The cable hat-band was introduced about 1599 ; and in the speech of Fastidio in " Every Man Out of His Humour," we find him saying : " I had a gold cable hat-band, then new come up, of massie goldsmith's work."
† " My mother . . . had rather follow me to the grave than see me tear my clothes, and hang down my head and sneak about with dirty shoes and blotted fingers, hair unpowdered and a hat uncocked." (Rambler, 109.) See also, Ashton, " Social Life in the Reign of Queen Anne," p. 107.
‡ Spectator, 319.

"Cynthia's Revels" we read: "Where is your page?
Call for your casting bottle, and place your mirror in
your hat, as I told you." This, however, was the height
of affectation. Ladies wore mirrors in their girdles,
and on their breasts; and Lovelace says:

> "My lively shade thou ever shalt retaine,
> In thy enclosèd, feather-framèd glasse." *

The cocked hat was universal, and was worn by boys
as well as men—the "tri-corne" of the French. The
varying cocks † were well known; there were, for instance, the "military cock," the "mercantile cock,"
the "Denmark cock"; they were ridiculed occasionally
as the "Egham, Staines and Windsor," from the three-
cornered sign post of that name. During this period
all hats were black, with a gold or silver band.

The London *Chronicle* (Vol. XI., p. 167, for the year
1762) has the following:

> Hats are now worn upon an average, six inches and three-
> fifths broad in the brim, and cocked between Quaker and Keven-
> huller. Some have their hats open before, like a church-spout,
> or the tin scales they weigh flower in; some wear them rather
> sharper, like the nose of a greyhound; and we can distinguish
> by the taste of the hat, the mode of the wearer's mind. There
> is the military cock, and the mercantile cock; and while the
> beaux of St. James wear their hats under their arms, the beaux
> of Morefield 'Mall wear theirs diagonally over the left or right
> eye. Sailors wear the sides of their hats uniformly tucked down
> to the crown, and look as if they carried a triangular apple-
> pasty upon their heads. . . . With Quakers it is a point of their
> faith not to wear a button or a loop tight up; their hats spread
> over their heads like a pent-house, and darken the outward man,
> to signify that they have the inward light.

---

* Thistleton–Dyer, "Domestic Folk Lore," p. 115.

† In the two-cocked hat originated our naval and military cocked hats
of modern uniform.

The " Kevenhuller " would seem to have been an exaggerated form of cock, for one writ-
ing in *The Connoisseur*, in 1754 (No.
36), had said of the women's hats in
that year: " They are more bold and
impudent than the broad-brimmed,
staring *Kevenhullers* worn a few years
ago by the men."

The " Kevenhuller."
(After Hogarth.)

The " Ladie's Advice to A Painter," in the *London
Magazine* for August, 1755, ran thus:

> Painter, once more shew thy art;
> Draw the idol of my heart;
> Draw him as he sports away,
> Softly smiling, sweetly gay;
> Carefully each mode express,
> For man's judgment is his dress.
> Cock his beaver neat and well,
> (Beaver size of cockleshell);
> Cast around a silver cord,
> Glittering like the polish'd sword.
> Let his wig be thin of hairs,
> (Wig that covers half his ears).

Toward the end of the century there were signs of a
change. In 1770 hats became round; in 1772 they rose
behind and fell before, as in the portraits of some of
the old worthies well known. The round hat that again
appeared after 1789, with highish crown and wide
brim, was the ancestor of the top hat of the nineteenth
century. In 1776, the period of the American Revolution, the popular hat in Paris was that " à la Suisse,"
known later as the " Alpine " hat. Parisian anglo-
maniacs preferred the " jockey," small and round.
Then there were hats " à la Hollandais,"and " à la
Quaker," both the latter round in form, with large

brim, usually worn in preference by the more old-fashioned. The French Revolution put a period to wigs, and hence also to the " chapeau bras "; for as a protection these enormous powdered periwigs rendered hats superfluous, beside the necessity for displaying what had been come at with such expenditure of time and money!

> " His pretty black beaver tucked under his arm,
>   If placed on his head, might keep it too warm ! "

After the great periwig disappeared, the " tie " wig followed, and then the " queue " of natural hair, with its neat ribbon bow, so familiar to us in the portraits of Washington and the men of the succeeding generation. The hat again became a necessity rather than a luxury, and resumed its place on the head. The beaver hat had a long life of two hundred years. Its weight was doubtless an element in its loss of popularity. For several years the " filled beaver " (a silk finish on a felt body, now obsolete), was worn; and by the early nineteenth century was leaving the cocked hat solely to conservative men of the older generation for full dress.

1810 saw the manufacture of the first all-silk hat. It did not become popular in Paris, and consequently anywhere else, until 1830. At that period the soft hat for purposes of dress was rejected, and the top hat came, and has never gone. At first it was the " Wellington," with " yeoman " crown; then the "Anglesea," with bell-shaped crown; then the D'Orsay, with ribbed silk binding and large bow on the band.* The American, like the Frenchman, has been largely released from

---

* Georgiana Hill, " History of English Dress. Vol. II., p. 254.

the dominion of the stiff hat for ordinary occasions; and this freedom is traceable to the influence respectively of the first Mexican war, when we made the acquaintance of the soft and picturesque Spanish hat; the rush of the " '49ers," who were again introduced to it, in California three years later; and the wild enthusiasm that greeted Kossuth when he first came to our shores wearing the " Alpine " hat and feather.* We drew the line at the feather, but his hat is with us still.

Such, briefly, is the history of the worldly hat, during two hundred years of Quakerism. Let us see what the Quaker did with his. The hat worn by Fox and ever since associated in our minds with the Quakers, was that of the cavalier, without the feather, worn less jauntily, but still the same. William Penn's more familiar figure will occur to us. Now it is easy to perceive that in a community where the people had been accustomed to see their older members retaining the hat much of the time while indoors, and had regarded the rapidly prevailing custom of removing it on entering the house as an affectation of the " smart set," that the moment any notion was suggested of the conscience being involved in the retention of that article, there would be a prompt response. Not only did the Quakers decline to greet their neighbors by doffing the hat, but they were equally stiff in the presence of the sovereign. Swift writes to Stella: " My friend Penn came here—

---

* This hat was much like the Welsh hat still worn, and the Tyrolese steeple hat. There was an old legend on the other side of the mountains, that the Tyrolese were men who wore such high-pointed hats that they could not walk about on the mountains without knocking down the stars. So the Lord God drew down the clouds every night to keep the stars in Heaven! The Spanish hat was somewhat the same. " Upon his head was a hat with a high peak, somewhat of the kind which the Spaniards call *calané*, so much in favor with the bravos of Seville and Madrid." George Borrow, " Romany Rye," p. 34.

Will Penn, the Quaker—at the head of his brethren, to thank the Duke for his kindness to their people in Ireland. To see a dozen scoundrels with their hats on, and the Duke complimenting with his off, was a good sight enough." * Charles II. once granted an audience to the courtly Quaker, William Penn, who, as was his custom, entered the royal presence with his hat on. The humorous sovereign quietly laid aside his own, which occasioned Penn's inquiry, " Friend Charles, why dost thou remove thy hat ? " " It is the custom," he replied, " in this place, for one person only to remain covered."

Apropos of Barclay's dictum in the Apology, " It is not lawful for Christians to kneel or prostrate themselves to any man," an observer of the English who traveled among them from the Continent in 1698, thus wrote, noting a slight improvement in the manners of the stricter Quakers at that date:

Plusieurs d'entre eux, depuis quelques années, s'humanisent un peu, a l'égard de la salutation; ils n'ôtent pas le chapeau, Dieu les garde de commetre cet horrible pêche: mais ils commencent à baiser un peu le menton, à faire une espèce de petite inclination de tête.

Old Tom Brown wrote:

These are more just than the other dissenters, because, as they pull not off their hats to God, so they pull them not off to men, whereas, the others shall cringe and bow to any man they may get sixpence by, but ne'er vail the bonnet to God, by whom they may get Heaven.†

Fox says:

Moreover, when the Lord sent me into the world, he forbade me to put off my hat to any, high or low, and I was required to thee and thou all men and women, without any respect to rich or poor, great or small. And as I travelled up and down, I was

---

* Journal to Stella. January 15, 1712.
† Quoted " Archæologia." Vol. XXVII., p. 51.

not to bid people Good-morrow or Good-evening, neither might
I bow or scrape with my leg to any one; this made the sects
and professions rage.

At the Launceston assizes, in 1656, Fox was brought
into court wearing his hat, with his companion, Edward
Pyot. He says:

We stood a pretty while with our hats on, and all was quiet.
I was moved to say, "Peace be amongst you." Judge Glyn, a
Welshman, then Chief Justice of England, said to the gaoler,
"What be these you have brought here into court ? " "Prisoners, my Lord," says he. "Why do you not put off your hats ? "
said the judge to us. We said nothing. "Put off your hats,"
said the Judge again. Still we said nothing. Then said the
Judge, "The court commands you to put off your hats." Then
I queried, "Where did ever any magistrate, king or judge, from
Moses to Daniel, command any to put off their hats, when they
came before them in their courts, either among the Jews, (the
people of God), or the heathen? and if the law of England doth
command any such thing, shew me that law, either written or
printed." The Judge grew very angry, and said, "I do not
carry my law-books on my back." . . . So they took us away,
and put us among the thieves. Presently after he said to the
gaoler, "Bring them up again." "Come," said he, "where had
they hats, from Moses to Daniel? Come, answer me, I have you
now." I replied, "Thou mayest read in the third of Daniel, that
the three children were cast into the fiery furnace by Nebuchad-
nezzar's command, with their coats, their hose and their hats
on." This plain instance stopped him; so that not having any
thing else to the point, he cried again, "Take him away,
gaoler."

In October, 1657, at Edinburgh, Fox was obliged to
appear before the Royal Council, and upon his entrance
into the Council Chamber the doorkeeper removed his
hat. "I asked him," says Fox, "why he did so, and
who was there, that I might not go in with my hat on?
I told him I had been before the Protector with my hat
on. But he hung up my hat and had me in before
them."

At Basingstoke, which Fox calls " a very rude town,"
he had a meeting, at the close of which he says: " I
was moved to put off my hat and pray to the Lord to
open their understandings; upon which they raised a
report that I put off my hat to them, and bid them
goodnight, which was never in my heart."   At Reading, 1658, he adds: " We had much to do with them
about our hats, and saying Thou and Thee to them.
They turned their profession of patience and moderation into rage and madness; many of them were like
distracted men for this hat-honour."   At the Exon assizes Friends were fined for not putting off their hats.
At Tenby, John-ap-John was imprisoned for wearing
his hat in what Fox calls " the steeple-house," which he
entered after leaving the meeting which Fox was at the
time conducting.   Next day, in a conversation with the
Governor, Fox says:

I asked him, " Why he cast my friend into prison ? "   He said,
" For standing with his hat on in the church."   I said, " Had not
the priest two caps on his head, a black one and a white one?
Cut off the brims of the hat, and then my friend would have but
one; and the brims of the hat were but to defend him from the
weather."   " These are frivolous things," said the Governor.
" Why, then," said I, " dost thou cast my friend into prison for
such frivolous things ? "

In London, before Sir Henry Vane, Friends were
finally admitted to court with their hats on, chiefly
through the mediation of others.

That so serious results should have followed so apparently innocent a peculiarity as the refusal to remove
the hat, or give what the Quakers termed " hat-honor,"
seems almost incredible to us now.   And doubtless
there were many in the position of Johnson's " pious

gentleman," who, though " he never entered a church, never passed one without taking off his hat." Robert Barclay sums up the whole matter when he says:

Kneeling, bowing and uncovering of the head is the alone outward signification of our adoration towards God, and therefore it is not lawful to give it unto man. He that kneeleth or prostrateth himself to man, what doeth he more to God? He that boweth and uncovereth his head to the Creature, what hath he reserved to the Creator ? *

It has been the mistake of writers upon costume not only to assert that the shape of the hat has never materially altered among the Quakers, but that they never wore cocked hats at all. That cocked hats accompanied the wigs, and were the usual form of head-dress at one time, even in the minister's gallery, is a perfectly established fact. George Dillwyn, who died in 1820, wears the transition hat, from the cock, to the broad-brim revived and modified. The broad-brim and the cock are the two forms of the Quaker hat. The common sense of the cock early appealed to the practical Quaker mind, and we have many portraits of prominent Quakers in hats of varying cock—Dr. Fothergill, Dr. Lettsom, William Cookworthy in England; and in America, Robert Proud, the Pembertons, Owen Jones, and many others. The Americans were always more strict in dress than the English, largely because his proximity to the continent familiarized the Englishman with more cosmopolitan ideas. However, the kind of cock was vastly important. Hannah Callowhill Penn, William Penn's second wife, in writing to her son Thomas Penn, in London, December, 1717, says:

* " Apology." Proposition XV.

I wish thou could have shifted till nearer Spring for a hatt, for I doubt to buy a good one now 'twill be near spoyled before the Hight of summer. . . . However, consider and act for the best Husbandry, and then please thyselfe; but be sure wch. ever 'tis, that 'tis packed up in a very Frd. like way, for the fantastical cocks in thine and thy brother Johne's hats has burthened my Spiritt much, and Indeed more than most of your Dress besides; therefore, as thou Vallues my Comfort, Regulate it more for the future. I have a Multitude of Toyls and Cares, but they would be greatly Mitigated, if I may but behold thee and thy Brother, persuing hard after Vertue and leaving as behind your backs the Toyish allurements and snares of this uncertain world.*

In spite of himself, the Quaker was carried along on the tide of fashion; indeed, he might to this day be

Owen Jones.
Colonial Treasurer of Penna.
Nat. 1711.   Obiit 1793.
Ae. 82.

wearing his heavy beaver hat, had it not, like the mammoth, become extinct! Certain of the "plainer sort" (not in the sense in which George Fox used the term, but meaning the more strict in guise) for many years refused to dye the beaver of their hats. The last white beaver hat did not disappear from Philadelphia until 1876, when what we know as the modern silk hat appeared.† A modification of it was adopted by the cosmopolitan Quaker, and has ever since been retained. To the initiated, however, the silk hat goes a long way to mark the man; and the decree of King Edward VII. in favor of that adornment, keeps it *de rigueur* in England

* Howard M. Jenkins, " The Family of William Penn," p. 99.
† John Hetherington wore the first silk top hat on the Strand, in London, in 1797. The style was his own invention, and he was mobbed in consequence.

JOHN PEMBERTON.

HENRY DRINKER.

JAMES PEMBERTON.

JOHN PARRISH.

Four Old-Time Pennsylvania Worthies.

John Pemberton, 1727-1795
Henry Drinker, 1734-1809.
James Pemberton, 1724-1809.
John Parrish, 1730-1807.

Septimus Roberts, 1807

Aged 18.

After the etching by Rosenthal.

and America. As the silk hat of the cabinet minister is not the mercantile silk hat, nor yet that of
the cleric, so the Quaker hat also retains its individuality; and in its shiny perfection and its amplitude
of dimensions, when mounted above the occasional
straight coat collar, more nearly resembles the dress
of the American Roman Catholic priest than any other.
The modern young Quaker has now freed himself
from the conventions of the early nineteenth century, and is often ignorant of the true reasons for the
peculiarities of his forefathers. When the court gallants of James II. lowered their crowns and widened

Puritan.   1653.

their brims, the Puritans kept their crowns high.
Charles II. escaped in a " very greasy old grey steeple-
crowned hat, with the brim turned up, without lining
or hat-band." The high-crowned hat was beginning to
be old-fashioned before his time; hence its choice as a
means of disguise. So tall a hat had had its inconveniences, as we read: " I pray, what were our sugar-loofe
hats, so mightily affected of late, both by men and
women, so incommodious for us, that every puffe of
winde deprived us of them, requiring the employment

of one hand to keep them on." * The tall hat came to
America on our Pilgrim Fathers, where its shape underwent a slight alteration. The brim became more
narrow, and the top rather less pointed. Difficulty in
finishing the beaver quite so finely also left the fur
more fluffy. We are told that this hat lasted in New
England until the time came for Benjamin Franklin
to go to France, when, as we know, he went to Paris
in a New England chimney-pot hat. This was at once
adopted by the ardent Parisians, who almost worshiped
the American envoy, as " anti-English," the symbol of
Liberty, etc. For some years the French had a monop-
oly of it; then it came to England, and eventually to
America again, transformed and modified into the
modern top hat. It may be noted that the Quakers
adopted the court style of James II., and not the Puritan hat, when they first wore the beaver, illustrating
in the hat, as has elsewhere been shown in their long
hair, the loyalty to the crown that was a part of their
conservatism. One of these early Quaker hats, once
the property of Reuben Macy, may now be seen in the
museum at Nantucket, Massachusetts.†

The attitude of the Quakers at once led to endless
controversies, whose repetition here is unnecessary.

---

* Bulwer, " Artificial Changeling." Quoted by Repton, in Archæologia. Vol. XXIV., p. 181.

† A French Canadian Journal of recent date (Montreal " Presse,"
ed. hebdomadaire, May 18th, 1899), thus describes with mild surprise
and courteously expressed admiration, a nineteenth century Friend who
has retained the plain garb of the latest form evolved. He is called
" un ministre Quaker," " d'une taille gigantesque." " Pour ne parler
que de sa coiffure, disons de suite qu'il portait un chapeau de castor de
dix-huit pouces de hauteur avec des bords droits d'égales dimensions.
. . . Il ne parle qu'à la seconde personne, et n'ôte son fameux couvre-
chef que *pour dormir !* En dehors de sa toquade réligieuse, dont il vous
entretient a l'exclusion de tout autre sujet, c'est un gentilhomme d'une in-
telligence remarkable."

Much literature appeared on the subject, which furnished a fruitful source to the writer of satirical tracts.
Such things were published as " Wickham Wakened:
or The Quakers Madrigal, in Rime Dogrell," beginning:

> The Quaker and his brats
> Are born with their hats,
> Which a point with two Taggs
> Ties fast to their Craggs.*

Certain Friends warned their members that the removal of the hat was a dangerous formality. During
worship, however, Fox had given instructions that the

Nantucket Beaver Hat.

head should be uncovered at time of prayer, and
Friends should either reverently kneel, as among the
Episcopalians, or stand, as did the Presbyterians. The
latter custom eventually became adopted.

The " Canons and Institutions " of Fox, in Article
Seventh, condemn " those who wear their Hattes when

---

* By Martin Llewellyn, of Christ Church, Oxford.

Friends pray." Fox was originally in the habit of attending the Church of England. When welcome doctrine was expounded, he removed his hat; if, however,
the preacher uttered unwelcome sentiments, he sol-
emnly put it on as a protest; and if the matter continued
to offend him, he rose and silently left. It was for
purposes of habitual protest that Quakers first learned
to sit in places of worship with their hats on. The protest was a decorous and inoffensive one, compared with
much of the rough dealing then prevalent. There was
no proper attitude of reverence in the London churches
up to, and during the time of Queen Anne; lolling, rising, or sitting at will being the rule, even among the
Episcopalians.* The Presbyterian minister's example
in the pulpit was so far followed, that often in country
neighborhoods, one might see the louts of the congregation fling on their hats in sermon time. In Scotland,
in 1740, a traveler condemns " a custom which I see
is getting pretty general among the lower sort, of cocking on the hat when the sermon began." William
Mucklow, who, in his " Spirit of the Hat," had said that
" the removal of the hat in worship and during prayer
is the beginning of a formal worship," was eventually
" recovered to a better mind," and brought to agree
with Fox and to be more in charity with Friends.
George Whitehead says,† "All preaching cannot be that
entire and peculiar prophesying, which, when one is immediately called to, I grant it is most seemly to stand
up with the hat off." Some others beside the Independents preached with the hat on. Lady Montague

---

* See Spectator, No. 455, and Tatler, No. 241.
† " The Apostate Incendiary Rebuked," p. 30.

wrote from Nimeguen, in the Netherlands, in 1716 [Letters]: " I was yesterday at the French church, and stared very much at the manner of the service. The parson clapped on a broad brimmed hat in the first place, which gave him the air of What d'ye call him, in Bartholomew Fair." Up to the middle of the eighteenth century, the hat was a prominent object in their pulpits. At a parish in Clydesdale (Scotland), the patron said to a new candidate for the incumbency, " Sir, there are two nails in the pulpit, on one of which the late worthy minister used to hang his hat. If you put your hat on the right one, it will please; none of the others have hit upon it." He did so, and got the place !* The clergy in the earliest days in England had worn woollen caps, which in some form long prevailed. The Scotch minister of 1700 was not so different from his congregation in dress as one hundred years later, when an official clerical uniform had been evolved and received general recognition. The cleric of the earlier date wore gray homespun, like his next neighbor, with a colored cravat; while in 1800, he appeared on Edinburgh streets, wearing a brown wig, or possibly powdered hair in a pigtail, a cocked hat, black single-breasted coat, frills and ruffles, knee-breeches and silver-buckled shoes, and bore himself with a general air of dignity that his predecessor would have regarded as savoring of worldliness to the last degree. Culture and religion, in those early days in Scotland, could never go hand in hand.

Martin Mason, of Lincoln, who was one of John Perot's schism in regard to taking off the hat in time

* H. G. Graham, " Social Life in Scotland in the Eighteenth Century." Vol. II., p. 104.

of prayer,* and who wrote verses to the memory of
Perot, says, in a letter to a friend, " What matter
whether Hat on or Hat off, so long as the Heart is
right ? " †

The majesty of the law demanded recognition in the
removal of the hat; and it was in the courts that Friends
suffered most severely because they could not conscien-
tiously observe the conventionalities.   The famous case
of William Penn and William Meade, the son-in-law of
Margaret Fox, may be cited as an early instance. After
their discharge by the jury at the trial, September 1-5,
1670, they were re-committed to Newgate in default
of payment of fines for " contempt of court " in declining to remove their hats during the trial.   Admiral
Penn paid their fines two days later, without their
knowledge, and they were released.   Thousands of
similar cases are to be found in England.   The feeling
was the same in New England.   But the presence of
Penn at the head of the administration of affairs in
Pennsylvania gave the Quakers in that colony a distinct
advantage in regard to some of their scruples.   After
his death, the traditions of his proprietaryship are well
exemplified in the following petition and the resulting
order of the Chancellor.   Sir William Keith, who filled
that office, instituted in 1720 a Court of Chancery,
and it was before that court that the eminent Chief Justice Kinsey appeared with his hat on.   John Kinsey
was prominent both as lawyer and Quaker, and when he

---

* Ellwood refers to Perot's " peculiar error of keeping on the Hatte
in Time of Prayer, as well publick as private, unless they had an immediate motion at that time to put it off."

† Joseph Smith, Catalogue of Friends' Books. Vol. II., p. 153. See
also, by Richard Richardson, of London, " Of adoration in general, & in
particular, of Hat-Honour—their rise, etc."   8vo, 1680.

followed the usual custom of his sect in retaining his hat, the President promptly ordered it taken off, which was accordingly done.* This arbitrary proceeding called forth

The humble address of the people called Quakers, by appointment of their Quarterly Meeting, held in Philadelphia, for the city and county, 2nd. of second month, 1725,—

May it please the Governor: Having maturely considered the inconveniences and hardships which, we are apprehensive, all those of our community may be laid under who shall be obliged or required to attend the respective courts of judicature in this province, if they may not be admitted without first having their hats taken off from their heads by an officer, as we understand was the case of our friend John Kinsey, when the Governor was pleased to command his to be taken off, before he could be admitted to speak in a case depending in a Court of Chancery, after that he had declared that he could not, for conscience, comply with the Governor's order to himself to the same purpose; which, being altogether new and unprecedented in this province, was the more surprising to the spectators, and as we conceive (however slight some may account it) has a tendency to the subversion of our religious liberties.

This province, with the powers of government, was granted by King Charles the Second to our proprietor, who, at the time of the said grant, was known to dissent from the national way of worship in divers points, and particularly in that of outward behavior, of refusing to pay unto man the honors that he, with all others of the same profession, believe only to be due to the Supreme Being; and they have, on occasions, supported their testimony, so far as to be frequently subjected to the insults of such as require that homage.

That the principal part of those who accompanied our said proprietor in his first settlement of this colony with others of the same profession, who have since retired into it, justly conceived that by virtue of said powers granted to our proprietor, they should have a free and unquestioned right to the exercise of their religious principles, and their persuasion in the aforementioned points and all others, by which they were distinguished from those of all other professions. And it seems

* Proud. Vol. II., p. 197.

not unreasonable to conceive an indulgence intended by the crown, in graciously leaving the government to him and them in such manner as may best suit their circumstances which appears to have been an early care in the first legislators, by several acts, as that of Liberty of Conscience, and more particularly by a law of the province, passed in the thirteenth year of King William, Chapter xcii, now in force. It is provided, "That in all courts, all persons, of all persuasions, may freely appear in their own way, and according to their own manner, and there personally plead their own cause, or, if unable, by their friends," which provision appears to be directly intended to guard against all exceptions to any person appearing in their own way, as our friend at the aforesaid court.

Now, though no people can be more ready and willing, in all things essential, to pay due regard to superiors, and honor the courts of justice, and those who administer them, yet, in such points as interfere with our conscientious persuasion, we have openly and firmly borne our testimony in all countries and places where our lot has fallen.

We must therefore, crave leave to hope, from the reasons here humbly offered, that the Governor, when he fully considers them, will be of opinion with us, that we may justly and modestly claim it as a right, that we and our friends should, at all times, be excused in the government from any compliances against our conscientious persuasions; and humbly request that he would, in future, account it so to us, thy assured, well-wishing friends.

Signed by appointment of the said meeting,

John Goodson,	Samuel Preston,	Morris Morris,
Rowland Ellis,	William Hudson,	Anthony Morris,
Reece Thomas,	Richard Hill,	Evan Evans.
Richard Hayes,		

On consideration had of the humble address presented, this day read in open court, from the Quarterly Meeting of the people called Quakers for the city and county of Philadelphia; it is ordered, that the address be filed with the Register, and that it be made a standing rule of the Court of Chancery for the Province of Pennsylvania for all time to come, that any practitioner of the law, or other officer or person, whatsoever, professing himself to be one of the people called Quakers, may, and shall be admitted, if they so think fit, to speak or otherwise officiate or apply themselves decently unto the said court without being obliged to observe the usual ceremony of uncovering their heads, by having their hats taken off. And such privilege, hereby ordered and granted to the people called Quakers, shall at no time hereafter be understood or interpreted as any contempt or neglect of said Court; and shall be taken only as an act of conscientious liberty, of right appertaining to the religious persuasion of the said people, and agreeable to their practice in all civil affairs of life.

BY SIR WILLIAM KEITH, Chancellor.*

The refusal of Fox and his contemporaries to remove their hats before Justices, etc., had not been a new thing in England. In Bishop Aylmer's time "there were a sort of people who counted it idolatry to pull off their hat or give reverence, even to princes." † These were probably a sect of the Anabaptists. Aylmer was Bishop of London between 1578 and 1594. The German Baptists refused the customary greetings.

This method of protest had been in use among other dissenters also, as the following instance from New England will serve to illustrate:

William Witter, of Lynn, Massachusetts, was an aged Baptist, who had already been prosecuted by the Puritans; but in 1651, being blind and infirm, he asked the Newport church to send some of the brethren to him, to administer the communion, for he found himself alone in Massachusetts. Accordingly, John Clark (the pastor) undertook the mission, accompanied by Obadiah Holmes and John Crandall.

They reached Lynn on Saturday, July 19, 1651, and on Sunday staid within doors, in order not to disturb the congregation. A few friends were present, and Clark was in the midst of a sermon, when the house was entered by two constables with a warrant signed by Robert Bridges, commanding them to arrest certain " erroneous persons being strangers." The travellers were at once seized and carried to the tavern, and after dinner they were told that they must go to church. . . . The unfortunate

---

* Michener, " Retrospect of Early Quakerism," p. 368.

† Robert Barclay, " Inner Life of the Religious Societies of the Commonwealth," p. 501.

Baptists remonstrated, saying that were they forced into the meeting house, they should be obliged to dissent from the service, but this the constable said, was nothing to him, and so he carried them away. On entering, during the prayer, the prisoners took off their hats, but presently put them on again and began reading in their seats. Whereupon Bridges ordered the officers to uncover their heads, which was done, and the service was then quietly finished. When all was over, Clark asked leave to speak, which, after some hesitation, was granted, on condition he would not discuss what he had heard. He began to explain how he had put on his hat because he could not judge that they were gathered according to the visible order of the Lord; but here he was silenced, and the three committed to custody for the night.[*]

After a violent struggle, the ministers under John Norton's lead succeeded, on the 19th of October, 1658, in forcing the capital act through the Legislature, which contained a clause making the denial of reverence to Superiors, or in other words, wearing the hat, evidence of Quakerism.[†]

This was at the time of the famous trial of the Southwicks.

We are told of four Quakers, who, on the 27th of Eighth month, 1658, at Boston, were brought before the General Court. They were Samuel Shattuck, N. Phelps, Joshua Buffum, and Ann Needham. George Bishop's account of their case as he addressed that Court is as follows:

They answered that they intended no Offense to you in coming thither (for they must come to you in their clothes, if they come decently, of which the hat is part) for it was not their Manner to have to do with Courts. And as for withdrawing from the Meetings, or keeping on their Hats, or doing anything in Contempt of them or their Laws, they said, the Lord was their Witness (as he is) that they did it not. So ye rose up and bid the Jaylor take them away.[‡]

The Puritan minister, John Wilson, at the hanging of the

---

[*] Brooks Adams, "The Emancipation of Massachusetts," p. 111.

[†] Ibid., p. 170.

[‡] George Bishop, "New England Judged," p. 85.

Quaker, William Robinson, on Boston Common, in 1659, said to the Quakers present, " Shall such Jacks as you come in before Authority with your Hats on ?" To which Robinson replied, " Mind you, mind you, it is for not putting off the Hat we are put to Death.*

Later on, the usual fine for keeping on the hat seems to have been twenty shillings. The long hair of the Quakers was an offence to the Puritans of Massachusetts, as well as to those on the other side of the Atlantic. Edward Wharton was a " turbulent Quaker," whose persecutions were related by George Bishop,† in reply to his inquiry of the Boston judges:

"Wherefore have I been fetch'd from my Habitation, where I was following my honest Calling, and here laid up as an Evil-Doer ?" "Your Hair is too long (reply'd you), and you are disobedient to that Commandment which saith, 'Honour thy Father and Mother.'" To which said Edward, "Wherein ?" "In that you will not put off your Hat, (said you) before the Magistrates."

The same Wharton, with four other Quakers, was brought before the General Court, Boston, 3 mo., 1665.

Their hats, (the great offence), were commanded to be taken off, and thrown on the Ground; which, being done, Mary Tomkins set her foot upon one of the Hats, and calling to you said, " See, I have your Honour under my Feet." Whereupon you demanded of her where her habitation was? She answered, " My Habitation is in the Lord." ‡

A feeling of irritation is hardly to be wondered at on the part of any judge who got no more direct reply from a prisoner than that of Mary Tomkins. But this was a trifling matter; for to bluff and confound the Jus-

---

* George Bishop, " New England Judged," p. 124.
† Ibid., p. 304. See also Brooks Adams, " The Emancipation of Massachusetts," p. 151.
‡ Ibid., p. 460.

tice was the proper method employed by all men in the English Courts of Law in that day, when literature shared in the involved style of intercourse and address, then universal. "Turbulent" was a term applied to these early Quakers by their contemporaries, and, indeed, by some of those contemporaries' descendants, who inherit still the old persecuting spirit.

Thomas Ellwood in 1660, when, as a youth, he was undergoing much for the sake of his hat, gives us a description of his costume that is most interesting to us now. He says:

> While I was in London, I went to a little meeting of Friends, which was then held in the House of one Humphrey Bache, a Goldsmith, at the Sign of the Snail, in Tower Street. It was then a very troublesome time, not from the Government, but from the Rabble of Boys and Rude People, who, upon the turn of the Times, (upon the return of the King) took Liberty to be very abusive.
>
> When the Meeting ended, a pretty Number of these unruly Folk were got together at the Door, ready to receive the Friends as they came forth not only with evil Words, but with Blows. . . . But quite contrary to my Expectation, when I came out, they said one to another, "Let him alone; don't meddle with him; he is no Quaker, I'll warrant you."
>
> I was troubled to think what the Matter was, or what these rude People saw in me, that made them not take me for a Quaker. And upon a close examination of myself, with respect to my Habit and Deportment, I could not find anything to place it on, but that I had then on my Head a large Mountier Cap of black Velvet, the Skirt of which being turned up in Folds, looked (it seems), somewhat above the common Garb of a Quaker; and this put me out of Conceit of my Cap.

Not long after this he writes:

> When a young Priest, who, as I understood, was Chaplain in (a certain) family, took upon him pragmatically to reprove me for standing with my Hat on before the Magistrates, and snatch'd my Cap from off my Head, Knowles (the Deputy-

Lieutenant) in a pleasant manner corrected him, telling him he mistook himself in taking a Cap for a Hat (for mine was a Mountier-Cap) and bid him give it me again; which he (though unwillingly) doing, I forthwith put it on my Head again, and thenceforward none meddled with me about it.

Again, he adds:

I had in my hand a little Walking-Stick with a Head on it. which he took out of my Hand to look on it; but I saw his Intention was to search it, whether it had a Tuck in it [sword] for he tried to have drawn the Head; but when he found it was Fast, he returned it to me.

The violent antipathy of Thomas Ellwood's father to any Quaker who refused to remove his hat in his presence, caused his son many painful scenes with the worthy squire, and an alienation that was a grief to both. One of these occasions is thus described by Ellwood:

The sight of my hat upon my head . . . (made) . . . his passion of grief turn to anger; he could not contain himself; but running upon me with both hands, first violently snatcht off my Hat and threw it away; and then giving me some buffets on the head he said, "Sirrah, get you up to your chamber." . . . I had now lost one of my hats, and I had but one more. That therefore, I put on, but did not keep it long; for the next Time my Father saw it on my Head, he tore it violently from me, and laid it up with the other, I knew not where. Wherefore I put on my Mountier-Cap, which was all I had left to wear on my head, and it was but a very little while that I had that to wear, for as soon as my Father came where I was, I lost that also. And now I was forced to go bareheaded wherever I had Occasion to go, within Doors and without.* . . .

The day that I came home I did not see my Father, nor until noon the next Day, when I went into the Parlour where he was, to take my usual Place at Dinner. As soon as I came in, I observed by my Father's Countenance, that my Hat was still an Offence to him; but when I was sitten down, and before I had

---

* " The History of the Life of Thomas Ellwood," by Himself; pp. 50–2, 3d ed. 1765.

eaten anything, he made me understand it more fully, by saying to me, but in a milder Tone than he had formerly used to
speak to me in, " If you cannot content yourself to come to Dinner without your Hive upon your Head [so he called my Hat],
pray rise and go take your Dinner some where else." Upon
those words, I arose from the Table, and leaving the Room, went
into the Kitchen, where I staid till the Servants went to Dinner, and then sate down very contentedly with them. . . . And
from this time he rather chose, as I thought, to avoid seeing me,
than to renew the Quarrel about the Hat.*

It appears that many wore caps and other varieties
of head dress at first among the Friends, for the broad-
brim was only just becoming sufficiently popular to be
safely adopted by them without any risk of seeming
too much in the mode. Moreover, they were all too
much engaged in preaching and in ministering to their
brethren who were in suffering from present or past
imprisonments, to devote much time to dress, and each
wore what best suited his purse and convenience. This
is fully demonstrated in a charming little incident related by Ellwood, who met the great young missionary,
Edward Burrough, on his way to Oxford. Burrough
was one of the early Quaker martyrs, dying in a foul
prison at the age of twenty-eight.

When I was come within a mile or so of the city (Oxford),
whom should I meet upon the way, coming from thence, but Edward Burrough! I rode in a Mountier (montero) cap (a dress
more used then than now), and so did he; and because the
weather was exceeding sharp, we both had drawn our caps down,
to shelter our Faces from the Cold, and by that means neither
of us knew the other, but passed by without taking notice one
of the other till a few Days after, meeting again, and observing each other's dress, we recollected where we had so lately
met.†

---

* " The History of the Life of Thomas Ellwood," by Himself; p. 68.
† Ibid., p. 31.

This was in the year 1659. The Century Dictionary defines a montero cap as derived from the Spanish "Montero, a hunter," and describes it as "a horseman's or huntsman's cap, having a round crown with flaps which could be drawn down over the sides of the face." *

But the cap, as time went on, had to be given up, for it was not very long before the broad-brim became unfashionable, and then it grew to be the distinctive mark of the Quaker. His following was so large that the hat became the badge of Quakerism wherever he went.

Thomas Story, the famous Quaker traveler and preacher, who became a member of Penn's Council of State, Master of the Rolls, and Commissioner of Claims in Pennsylvania, describes graphically in his Journal the sufferings he endured as a young man on the subject of the hat; his treatment by his father was quite similar to that of Penn and Ellwood. All three were brought up as refined young men, carefully instructed by solicitous parents in all the airs and graces of polite society when it demanded far more formality and elaboration of manner than these busy, telephonic times will now permit their descendants. He tells us that in 1691 he was invited to meet some gentlemen at a tavern, and says:

I was not hasty to go, looking for the Countenance of the Lord therein, neither did I refuse; but my Father & some others, being impatient to have me among them, came likewise to me. I arose from my seat when they came in, but did not move my

---

* "His hat was like a Helmet, or Spanish *Montero*," (Bacon). Evelyn's "Tyrannas" calls the Montero "light and serviceable when the sun is hot, and at other times ornamental."

Hat to them as they to me. Upon which my Father fell a weep-
ing and said, I did not use to behave so to him. I intreated
him not to resent it as a Fault, for Tho' I now thought fit to
decline that Ceremony, it was not in Disobedience, or Disrespect
to him or them; for I honoured him as much as ever, and desired he would please to think so, notwithstanding exterior
Alteration.*

Of course it is possible to multiply indefinitely inci-
dents that show the struggles of the spirit in terms of
the hat. This affected even political questions, as well
as those social and religious; yet no more innocent body
of people ever walked the earth than they under the
broad-brims. In 1801 Richard Jordan, a well-known
American minister of the Society, was traveling on the
Continent with Abraham Barker, a Friend from New
Bedford, Massachusetts, and the party arrived in Paris.
Richard Jordan mentions the following incident in his
Journal:

It may not perhaps be amiss to mention how we were treated
at the municipality, where we attended to present our passports.
We were stopped by the guards, who had strict orders, it seems,
not to suffer any man to pass unless he had what is called a
cockade in his hat, but on our desiring our guide to step forward and inform the Officers that we were of the people called
Quakers, and that our not observing those signs of the times
was not in contempt of authority, or disrespect to any office,
but from a religious scruple in our minds,—it being the same
with us in our own country—they readily accepted our reasons;
and one of the officers came and took us by the guards, and so
up into the chamber, where we were suffered to remain quietly
with our hats on, until our passports were examined by two
officers, and again endorsed under the seal of the republic, permitting us to go to Calvisson, in Languedoc. Thus it often appears to me that we make our way better in the minds of the

---

*Thomas Story, Journal, p. 40. (Folio ed.)

people when we keep strictly to our religious profession, in all countries and among all sorts of persons.*

Joseph John Gurney relates his own experience upon the first occasion that his Quakerism affected his hat. The step was very marked for one who had not previously been a pronounced Friend, and who was so much in the midst of worldly interests as were all the Gurneys. He says:

> I was engaged long beforehand to a dinner party. For three weeks before I was in agitation from the knowledge that I must enter the drawing-room with my hat on. From this sacrifice, strange and unaccountable as it may seem, I could not escape. In a Friend's attire and with my hat on, I entered the drawing-room at the dreaded moment, shook hands with the mistress of the house, went back into the hall, deposited my hat, and returned home in some degree of peace. I had afterward the same thing to do at the Bishop's. The result was that I found myself a decided Quaker, was perfectly understood to have assumed that character, and to dinner parties, except in the family circle, I was asked no more.

This was in 1810, when the Quaker " testimony " had become but an eccentricity to the world, which chose to laugh rather than make it a cause for persecution. Samuel Gurney and his brother Joseph John possessed in a remarkable degree the physical beauty that so distinguished the family, and the black velvet cap worn in later life by the latter over his beautiful hair, then growing gray, gave him the air of a fine old Roman Catholic Archbishop.

It was no easy matter for the Quakers at any period thus to mortify the flesh, and Barclay says for himself and all his brethren:

---

* Richard Jordan, Journal, p. 106.

This I can say boldly in the sight of God, from my own experience & that of many thousands more, that however small or foolish this may seem, yet we behooved to suffer death rather than do it, [i.e., remove the hat] and that *for conscience' sake;* and that, in its being so contrary to our natural spirits, there are many of us to whom the forsaking of these bowings and ceremonies was as death itself; which we could never have left if we could have enjoyed our peace with God in the use of them.

Royalist Hat, time of Commonwealth.
(After Martin.)

CHAPTER III.

BEARDS, WIGS AND BANDS.

Now a beard is a thing that commands in a King
  Be his sceptres never so fair ;
Where the beard bears the sway, the people obey,
  And are subject to a hair.
  .   .   .   .

Now of the beards there be such a company,
  And fashions such a throng,
That it is very hard to handle a beard,
  Tho' it be never so long.

Ballad of the Beard, Temp. Ch. I.

William Penn.

After the bust in ivory by Sylvanus Bevan.

CHAPTER III.

I T happened that Quaker customs began to crystallize at a time when smooth faces were universal; and to this accident is due their later " testimony " against beards, which would have been quite as strong against the practice of shaving off a natural adornment had the sect arisen a century earlier. It was noted by the early historian Sewel, as one of John Perot's " extravagant steps," that he had allowed his beard to grow! Portraits of James Nayler, the " Apostate," show him in a full pointed beard; and there are also prints of the early Quaker preachers with flowing beards, but they are conspicuous exceptions. The full beard of Henry IV. had by 1628 become the pointed beard. Quicherat states as the origin of the smooth face the sportive order of Louis XIII. to his courtiers to cut off all the beard, leaving only a small tuft on the chin.* The Russians were conspicuous exceptions to this fashion; and Evelyn, under date 24 October, 1681, writes of the Russian Ambassador at the court of St. James: " 'Twas reported of him he condemned his sonn to lose his head

---

* The following verse celebrates this :
" Helas ! Ma pauvre barbe,
Qu'est-ce qui t'a faite ainsi?
C'est le grand roy Louis,
Treizième de se nom,
Qui toute a ésbarbé sa maison."

for shaving off his beard and putting himselfe in ye French fashion at Paris, and that he would have executed it had not the French King interceded."

The beard disappeared when the ruff went out, and smooth faces are associated with the time of the early Quakers, and the reign of the Stuarts. The moustache was not then fashionable, hence that military appendage did not have occasion to meet the disapproval of the Quakers until long after; and I have nowhere found any notice taken of the moustache in any meeting so far. Early in the present century an English fashion book remarks: "Young bucks have mounted the 'Jewish mustachio' on the upper lip." Parton says: "It is hard to believe in the soundness of a person's judgment who turns his collar down, when every one turns it up, or who allows his hair to grow long, when the rest of mankind wear theirs short." * Even more attention has been paid to the morality, so to speak, of the hair, than to that of the beard. Political opinions expressed themselves with the revolutionary party in England in the short hair of the Roundheads. The Puritans, therefore, are to be found with short locks, making religious capital out of what were really their political sympathies. The early Quakers, always conservative, and never, like the Irish, " agin the Government," wore the long hair of the Royalists (as did the French) for some years for fear of resemblance to the rebels. A notice published in 1698 mentions a delinquent Quaker " wearing his own hair straight and lank." The Germans wore unkempt beards and moustaches. The clergy, like the Quakers,

---

* James Parton, " The Clothes Mania."

have always been rigid in their ideas of dress, and even in the time of Stephen did not wear long hair or beards. Wigs, also, which appeared for a short time then, were later condemned, along with flowing locks. By 1487 they were wearing long beards, as in earlier times, but they were condemned for wearing long hair, and charged to cut it " short enough to show the ears." Carefully curled and powdered hair was the forerunner of the periwig. The clergy held out longest against adopting it, and were the last to discard it, except professors of the law. The first cleric to wear an official wig was Archbishop Tillotson, in the reign of James II. Once introduced, the wig was worn until the time of the French Revolution, just before which a fine wig cost thirty to forty guineas. Bishop Blomfield first set the example of wearing his own hair. Archbishop Sumner wore a wig so late as 1858, at the wedding of the Princess Royal. The church has now discarded the wig entirely, while the law is the only profession that retains it. The Speaker of the House of Commons is most imposing in a full-bottomed wig, while short wigs are worn by judges and barristers. The court coachmen and some of the servants of the nobility still wear the wig as a part of the livery.

King Charles the Second, lax as he was in his own person and costume, and wearing perhaps the heaviest periwig in the realm, had, nevertheless, certain notions of what was befitting the clergy. We read:

A letter was written by [him] to the University of Cambridge, forbidding its members to wear periwigs, smoke tobacco, or read their sermons; and when he was at Newmarket, Nathaniel Vincent, Doctor of Divinity, Fellow of Clare Hall, and Chaplain to his Majesty, preached before him in a long periwig and Holland sleeves, according to the fashion in use among gentlemen at that time. This foppery displeased the King, who commanded the Duke of Monmouth, then Chancellor of the University, to cause the statutes concerning decency of apparel to be put in execution, which was accordingly done.*

Thomas Story, the well-known Quaker preacher and traveler, relates † the following that was told him of Peter the Great, after that monarch had attended a Meeting of the Quakers at Friedrichstadt (Holstein) in 1712. The Czar was at one time attending a meeting held in a Dutch market place:

Being rainy Weather, when they were at it, the Czar wearing his own Hair, pulled off the great Wigg from one of his Dukes, and put it on himself, to Cover him from the Rain, making the owner stand bareheaded the while, for it seems he is so absolute, that there must be no grumbling at what he does, Life and Estate being wholly at his Discretion.

The portraits of George Fox show him with long locks, reaching to the shoulder, but he never wore a wig; while on the contrary, William Penn wore as many as four in one year. On the subject of his own long hair, Fox speaks occasionally in his Journal. In 1655, when before Major Ceely, during a journey into Cornwall, he says of the Major:

He had with him a silly young priest, who asked us many frivolous questions; amongst the rest, he desired to cut my hair which was then pretty long; but I was not to cut it, though many were offended at it. I told them I had no pride in it, and it was not of my own putting on.

A few months later, at Bristol, when Fox stood in the orchard that seems to have been a favorite meeting place for both Baptists and Quakers, addressing some thousands of people from the great stone that did duty

---

* "The Book of Costume, By A Lady of Quality." London, 1846.
† Thomas Story, Journal, p. 496. (Folio.)

as a pulpit, a certain " rude, jangling Baptist " began to find fault with Fox's long hair; but, he adds, " I said nothing to him." The following year, in Wales (1657), Fox's Journal records:

Next morning one called a Lady sent for me, who kept a preacher in her house, but I found both her and her preacher very light and airy; too light to receive the weighty things of God. In her lightness she came and asked me, " If she should cut my hair ? " I was moved to reprove her, and bid her cut down the corruptions in herself with the sword of the spirit of God; so after I had admonished her to be more grave and sober, we passed away. Afterward in her frothy mind, she made her boast that she " came up behind me and cut off the curl of my hair "; but she spoke falsely.

The fascinations of the wig proved too much for the other Quakers, however, and it soon became quite general among them, as the records of many old meetings testify. In 1698 periwigs on men and high headdresses on women are condemned. By 1717 so great a declension in plainness of dress had taken place, that a paper on " Pride, Plainness of Dress," etc., was issued by London Quarterly Meeting. This document inveighs against " men's extravagant Wigs and wearing the hair in a beauish manner "; it grants that " modest, decent or necessary (!) " wigs might be allowed; but prevailing modes are condemned. Some of the old Friends, in 1715, mourned, with good reason, we should think, that " some of the young people cut off good heads of hair to put on long extravagant, gay wigs." The periwig—" falbala," or " furbelow," the dress wig of the reign of Queen Anne—was the culmination of the art of dress in the life time of the second generation of Quakers. Ashton tells us that it was the invention of a French courtier to conceal a defect in the shoulders of the Duke of Burgundy. Its use spread all over Europe, and came to America. The true antiquarian holds everything worth preserving merely because it has been preserved. Hence we are blessed with the long list of the Kings' fools of old times, and among them we find that of Saxton, the Court fool of Henry VIII., who is the first person in modern England recorded to have worn a wig. In an account of the Treasurer of the King's Chambers in that reign is the entry: "Paid for Saxton, the King's fool, for a wig, 20s." *

The first official notice to be found of the wig among the early Quakers is in 1691, when London Six Weeks Meeting issued a "testimony" against "those that have imitated the world, whether it be men, in their extravagant periwigs, or modes in their apparel; or whether it be women in their high towering (head) dress, gold chains, or gaudy attire; or whether it be parents, like old Ely, not sufficiently restraining their children therefrom; . . . or whether it be in voluptuous feasting without fear, or costly furnitures, and too rich adorning of houses," etc.†

The "Wigges" may well have been called extravagant. An advertisement of Queen Anne's time, not many years before this, appeared in London, to the effect that on a certain public coach, "Dancing shoes not exceeding four inches in height, *and periwigs not exceeding three feet* (!) *in length,* are carried in the coach box gratis !" ‡ One of the dangers of London streets in that uncomfortable period of their history has been noticed by the poet Gay:

---

* Walpole, " Anecdotes of Painting " ; 3d ed., Vol. I., p. 135.
† Beck and Ball, " History of London Friends' Meetings," p. 117.
‡ Ashton, " Social Life in the Reign of Queen Anne," p. 109.

You'll sometimes meet a fop of nicest tread,
Whose mantling peruke veils his empty head.

. . . .

Him, like the miller, pass with caution by,
Lest from his shoulder clouds of powder fly.

. . . .

Nor is the flaxen wig with safety worn;
High on the shoulder, in a basket borne,
Lurks the sly boy, whose hand to rapine bred,
Plucks off the curling honors of the head.*

The wearing of wigs among the Quakers must have
been much more common than has been supposed, particularly with those somewhat fashionably inclined, if
we may judge from the large number of minutes and
other papers against that vanity, as well as the many
allusions to them in letters of an early date. William
Cookworthy and Doctors Fother-
gill and Lettsom have already been
instanced in describing their
cocked hats. William Dillwyn,
in both America and England,
wears a rather smaller wig than
theirs.

The care of the wig was a serious matter, and in every way its
use was in direct opposition to
Quaker principles of moderation
and economy. It is therefore the
more striking to discover how uni-

William Dillwyn.
1805.

* "Trivia." The "Ladies' Answer" to a ballad ridiculing black
hats and capuchins (published by Percy Soc., Vol. XXVII., p. 205),
thus remonstrated with the men :

"I wonder what these men can mean
To trouble their heads with our capuchins?
Let 'em mind their ruffs and mufetees :
Pray, what harm in our black hats is found,
To make them so much with scandal abound?
Why can they not let the women alone,
When idle fashions they have of their own?
With ramelie wigs and muffetees."

versally it was worn by the Friends, completely refuting
Miss Hill's statement that the Quakers never wore wigs.
For a time it was not considered decent or respectable
to appear in public without one; and the Quakers were
really less conspicuous by yielding to public opinion,
than if they had opposed it more strenuously. As in
the case of the adoption of pantaloons, the pressure of
circumstances was too much for them; although we find
them slow to adopt the wig, and, contrary to their usual
custom in matters of dress, among the first to discard
it. The wig was expensive, demanding a great deal of
time and money in its proper care; it was heavy and
awkward, and very messy and dirty, particularly when
powdered; and the periwig in the hands of a careless
person became a positive source of danger. What
would a modern Board of Health have said to Pepys'
entry in his Diary, under date September 3d, 1665?

Put on my coloured silk suit very fine and my new periwigg,
bought a good while since but durst not wear, because the plague
was in Westminster when I bought it. It is a wonder what will
be the fashion after the plague is done, as to periwiggs, for nobody will dare to buy any haire, for fear of the infection, that it
had been cut off of the heads of people dead of the plague.

Foulis, of Ravelston, Scotland, in 1704, pays "for
a new long periwig, 7 guineas and a halfe." His dress
wig costs " 14, 6s." Scots, or a guinea; a new hat, 7
Scots; a bob-wig, a guinea.* Allan Ramsay, the poet,
was a Jack-of-all-trades as well, and among other
things, he made wigs and " barberized " customers in
his night-cap. A friend of his, who was a Scotch judge,
put his wig in a sedan-chair to keep it dry from the

---

*H. G. Graham, " Social Life in Scotland in the Eighteenth
Century."

rain, and himself quietly walked home. The umbrella was still in the future; and a powdered periwig in a hard rain meant a ruined pocket book, and a head weighed down with a load of paste, drying into a mould of plastered hair! Therefore Gay's timely advice:

> When suffocating mists obscure the morn,
> Let thy worst wig, long used to storms be worn;
> This knows the powdered footman, and with care
> Beneath his flapping hat secures his hair.*

The " wigge," however, had come to stay. Through the whole of the eighteenth century it prevailed. The " Ranelagh Tail " was the beginning of the end, so to speak, toward the period of the American Revolution, as is seen in the portraits of some of the English officers of that time; the Americans, like Washington, usually preferring to wear their own hair tied with a ribbon in a knot behind, and occasionally powdered; the fashionable use of powder disappeared about 1794. Napoleon wore his queue and " cadenettes " in the campaign in Italy, sacrificing both in Egypt, where he prided himself on being unique among his Generals, who flattered his fancied resemblance, with short hair, to Titus. The " cadenette " † was worn well over the left ear, to which the gallants attached a large jewel.

---

* " Trivia."

† " Cadenette." So called from Maréchal Cadenet, of France, in the seventeenth century. The Century Dictionary defines it as " a love-lock, or tress of hair worn longer than the others."

> " L'ondoyant et venteux pennache
> Donnant du galbe à ce bravache,
> Un long flocon de poil natte
> En petits anneaux frisottes
> Pris au bout de tresse vermeille
> Descendoit de sa gauche oreille." *

---

* Quoted by Quicherat, " Histoire de Costume en France," p. 475.

This may be seen in the portrait of Charles I. in the Louvre, who wears a large pearl.

The English ladies wore the wig devotedly, probably for the same good reason that moved Mrs. Pepys. Her husband says (March 13, 1665): " My wife began to wear light locks, white almost, which, though it made her look very pretty, yet not being natural, vexes me, that I will not have her wear them." After the Brighton races, the bellman once gave notice to the inhabitants of that place that a lady had lost a wig coming from Broadwater. A reward offered brought no evidence of it. A great while after a bird's nest was discovered in a tree by some boys, who, climbing to seize the treasure, were surprised to find the lost wig, containing a few sticks, and the maker's name intact. We are also told of the discovery of a hedgehog's nest in the lost scratch wig of a toper, who dropped it along the roadside ! Thomas Ellwood had his opinion of the women who wore wigs, and did not hesitate to express it in most forcible, if not melodious, strains. The friend of Milton really waxed indignant:

> "Some Women (Oh the Shame!) like ramping Rigs,
> Ride flaunting in their powder'd Perriwigs;
> Astride they sit (and not ashamed neither)
> Drest up like men in Jacket, Cap and Feather ! " *

Lady Suffolk (Letters; 1728) says:

Mrs. Berkeley drives herself in a chair in a morning gown, with a white apron, a white handkerchief pinned under her head like a nun, a black silk over that, and another white one over the hat!

Nugent (Travels; 1766) describes the Duchess of Mechlenburg-Schwerin in " a riding-habit, with a bag-

---

* Thos. Ellwood, " Speculum Seculi ; or a Looking Glass for the Times."

wig, and a cocked hat and a feather." He several times tells us: "The ladies do wear hats and bag-wigs." The "Life and Actions of John Everett" (1729-30), tells us that "The Precisions" (as he calls the Quakers), "for the most part, though they are plain in their dress, wear the best of commodities, and though a smart toupie is an abomination, yet a bob or a natural of six or seven guineas' price, is a modest covering allowed of by the saints."

It is probable that the Quakers affected the "bob" wig chiefly. This style of wig was not intended for full dress, and the following instance, mentioned by Swift,* will well illustrate the distinctions in wig-wearing:

As Prince Eugene was going with Mr. Secretary to Court, he told the Secretary that Hoffman, the Emperor's resident, said to his Highness that it was not proper to go to Court without a long wig, and his was only a tied up one. "Now," says the Prince, "I know not what to do, for I never had a long periwig in my life; and I have sent to all my valets and footmen to see whether any of them have one, that I might borrow it, but none of them has any." But the Secretary said it was a thing of no consequence, and only observed by gentlemen ushers.

John Byrom, on the appearance of the President of a Club in a "black bob-wig" wrote:

"A phrensy? or a periwigmanee,
That overruns his pericranie ?" †

The father of Stephen Grellet, an officer in the court of Louis XVI., wears a "cauliflower" wig, as shown in his silhouette.

---

*Swift, "Journal to Stella," January 1, 1712.

† Leslie Stephen, "Studies of a Biographer," p. 91.

The American Puritans in the time of Charles I., issued a manifesto against long hair in their colony, calling it " an impious custom and a shameful practice for any man who has the least care for his soul to wear long hair." They enact that it shall be cropped and not worn in churches so that those persons who persist in this custom " shall have both God and man at the same time against them." * The Puritans permitted their people to wear out the clothes they brought with them, after which the sumptuary laws of Massachusetts went into force. These ordered that no slashed clothes were to be worn, but that one slash in each sleeve might be permitted! Beaver hats were prohibited. " Immoderate great shoes " were condemned, and four years later short shoes are also condemned as leading to " the nourishing of pride and exhausting men's estate." In 1651 the Government was solicitous to preserve the distinctions of rank; men must not be too richly dressed, nor wear " points " (ribbons with jeweled ends to tie up the clothing, often very gay) at the knee. Women with an income under two hundred pounds were not to wear silk or tiffany hoods. Long hair was condemned by the Legislature, and by the Grand Jury; while with a curious disregard for consistency, the women were condemned who cut and curled theirs. Evidently the modern prejudice against long-haired men and short-haired women is not so new. Wigs also fell under condemnation, but they prevailed by the end of the seventeenth century, despite the Fathers.

The sumptuary laws of the early Massachusetts col-

* See also " Dialogue between Captain Long-Haire and Captain Short-Haire." Brit. Mus. Harleian MSS. Pub. by Percy Soc. Vol. XXVII., p. 170.

onists are much like the orders of the Quakers to their constituency a little later. What must be emphasized all through this study of the Quaker idea of dress is the fact that their attention to plainness, and to all the details of every day life, was a natural reaction from dogmatism, royal prerogative and worldly extravagance. It was by no means a characteristic of the Quakers alone, but was even more pronounced among the Separatists, the Mennonites, and the Puritans; and of the latter body, none were so arbitrary or narrow as those who sought religious freedom in America. This is not the place for large quotations from the laws of the Massachusetts Colony. But it was the temper of the times which led Puritan and Quaker alike, whether in England, Holland or America, to attempt to rule the consciences of the people in minor matters of daily life, and thus to narrow the spiritual outlook of a whole sect. The other bodies threw off these small peculiarities, as the exigencies of the time in New England, for instance, demanded an active participation in the life— political and social—of the growing commonwealth. The Quakers in Pennsylvania, on the contrary, after 1756, the period of their withdrawal from the public arena, no longer participated in the political and social developments of the most rapid period of growth in that colony; they thereby preserved many little peculiarities of their most conservative sect, which peculiarities would necessarily have been rubbed off in contact with men of other minds. This must be borne in mind regarding the Quakers; for the same method of treatment would have preserved Puritan customs to us as interesting religious fossils to the present day.

Wigs were denounced in the Massachusettts legislature as early as 1675. John Eliot said that the wars and disturbances in the Puritan Meeting House were a judgment on the people for wearing wigs; * and he reluctantly acknowledged that " the lust for wigs is become insuperable ! " We know that John Wilson and Cotton Mather wore them. A young woman of Rhode Island, named Hetty Shepard, when visiting Boston, in 1676, wrote in her diary:

> I could not help laughing at the periwig of Elder Jones, which had gone awry. The periwig has been greatly censured as encouraging worldly fashions not suitable to the wearing of a minister of the Gospel, and it has been preached about by Mr. Mather, and many think he is not severe enough in the matter, but rather doth find excuse for it on account of health.†

Pepys records the first time he put on his wig, which was in 1663. By 1716 they were universal, although in 1722 the Puritans declared at Hampton that " ye wearing of extravagant, superfluous wigges is altogether contrary to Truth." The New York Assembly taxed every wig of human or horse hair mixed. The early Colonists, both Baptists and Friends, in 1689-1698, unitedly attacked the wearing of periwigs in men and high headdresses in women, the former holding that the anticipated appearance of the Fifth Monarchy made such frivolity both unnecessary and inappropriate. Portraits of Endicott, Judge Sewall, and others who abjured the wig, show them in small black skullcaps. The Judge, who wore a hood, probably did so to afford his neck the protection that the wearers of wigs

---

* W. R. Bliss, " Side Glimpses from the Colonial Meeting-house," p. 97.
  † Ibid. P. 136.

Moses Brown, 1738-1836.

Engraved by *T. Pollock, after the portrait by W. J. Harris.*

enjoyed with that vanity, and which in the bleak New England climate gave the custom more semblance of sense than anywhere else. The portrait of Moses Brown, the well-known Quaker of Providence, shows him in a similar substitute for the wig.

One of the earliest Quaker minutes in New England relating to the subject of wigs, occurs at Dartmouth, Massachusetts, whose Monthly Meeting records, under date First month 21, 1719: " A concern lying on this meeting Concerning of Friends Wearing of Wigs is referred to be proposed to the next Quarterly Meeting." Soon after, at the suggestion of the Yearly Meeting at Philadelphia, New England Yearly Meeting advised (1721) that the important subject of wigs be taken up. As a consequence of this action, in Sixth month of that year, Dartmouth Monthly Meeting appointed John Tucker and Thomas Taber, Jr., " to draw up something relating to wigges "; and Sandwich Quarterly Meeting, on First month 19, 1722, saw fit to elaborate its views as follows:

The Sense and Judgment of Sandwich Quarterly Meeting in Relation to Wigs is that if any friend by reason of Age or Sickness have lost their Hair, may wear a small decent Wig as much like their owne Hair as may be—but for any friend to cut of their Hair on purpose to wear a Wig seems to be more pride than Profit and when any professing truth with us go into the same, they ought to be proceeded against as disorderly walkers.

There is evidence of many who became so far " disorderly walkers " as to be quite unable to resist the fascinations of an artificial superstructure. The same meeting records some years later:

1 mo. 1791: R—— D—— hath given way to the Lust of the Eye and the Pride of Life in following some of the vain Fations and Customs of the times and Continues Therein; Especially that

of waring his Hair long which is a shame according to the Apostles Declaration; also tied with a string [doubtless the worldly
black ribbon worn by the Father of his Country, an example
for all loyal citizens to follow] and some other modes that we
have not unity with; also attended a marriage out of the order
of Friends; for all which we have Labored with him.

This case shows the period of transition from the wig
to the natural hair worn long, tied and powdered. Nantucket Records, dated Seventh month 6, 1803, also re-
late that F. H. " has deviated from our principles in
dress, particularly in tying the hair."

Dartmouth Meeting, in 1733 (Tenth month 17)
showed its sorrow for one of its members " going from
education " in the following minute:

Whereas, H—— T—— . . . hath had his Education among
Friends but for want of keeping the Spirit of Truth and ye good
order Established among Friends, hath gone from Education & let
himself into a Liberty that is not agreeable to our Holy Profession, by wearing Divers sorts of Periwigs and his Hat set up on
three sides like ye Vain Custom of ye World, and also Speaking
of Words not agreeable to our Profession, & for these his out-
goings he has been Labored with and Advised to forsake the
same, but he hath not done it to ye Satisfaction of ye Monthly
Meeting, but still goes on with his vain conversation, to the
grief of (the) sincere-hearted among us. Therefore for the clear-
ing of Truth of Such Reproachful things we are concerned to
give Forth this as a Public Condemnation.

Philadelphia, now the most conservative, was at that
period the most fashionable town in the new country,
and we find its Quaker Meeting struggling with the
wig-mania some time before there is any record of its
appearance among that body in New England. Such
minutes as the following are not uncommon:

It being spoken to at this Meeting as a grief upon some
friends, That many comes out of England with fashionable
Cloathes and great Perriwigs, which, if care be not taken may

(its feared) tend to Corrupt the Youth of this place. This Meeting recommends the same [to the next Quarterly Meeting.] —Philadelphia Monthly Meeting, 26 of 2 mo. 1700.

The friends appointed by the preparative Meeting to bring in the testimony of Ancient Friends concerning fashionable cloathing and Long Perriwigs, have done it, and they are desired to recommend the same to the next Quarterly Meeting.—Do., 30 of 3 mo. 1701.

Likewise the Friends appointed to Enquire into the Conversation and Clearness of Abraham Scott, Report that they cannot find but that he is clear in relation to marriage and debts, but as to his orderly walking amongst Friends, they cannot say much for him on that account. Yet upon his appearance before this meeting, making some acknowledgment of *Extraordinary Powdering of his Periwig*, which is the chief (thing) Friends had against him, and hoping to take more care for the future, Samuel Carpenter and Anthony Morris are desired to write him a Certificate and sign the same on behalf of this Meeting.—Do., 25 of 5 mo. 1701.

Under the same date we find:

Some course might be taken with the Taylors that make profession of Truth, and are found in the practice of making such fashionable cloathing as Tends to the Corruption of Youth.

They do not seem, however, to have gone the lengths of Dublin Meeting:

28 of 6 mo. 1702; Philadelphia Monthly Meeting desires that the proposition of the last Preparative meeting about cutting of hair & wearing of perriwigs, may be laid before the next Quarterly Meeting. . . . 17th. of 6 mo. 1703; Ordered that friends in their particular meetings make inquiry if there be any in the use of perriwigs extravagantly or unnecessary.

We also find the following, in an Epistle of Philadelphia Yearly Meeting to the Quarterly and Monthly Meetings, dated Seventh month 18, 1723, " on third day as usual ":

As to such young people who have been educated in the way of Truth, or make profession with us, if they do not continue

in well doing, but frequent scandalous or tipling houses, and
delight in vain and evil company and communications or shall
use gaming, or drink to excess, or behave rudely or such like
enormities or shall decline our plain manner of speech or imitate the vain antick modes and customs of the times—the men
with their extravagant wigges, and hattes set up with three
corners; and the women in their immodest dresses, and other
indecencies. It is our advice and earnest desire that parents and
guardians, whilst such youth are under their tuition, do restrain
them, and not indulge or maintain them in such pride or extravagances. But if they will not be otherwise reformed, then
the Overseers or other Frd's shall use their endeavours to restrain them, and if that cannot prevail, let the offenders (after
dealing and admonitions), have notice to be at the next succeeding monthly meeting, in order to be further dealt withall
in the Wisdom of Truth, according to the Discipline.

It is a curious fact that wigs were discarded with
more apparent reluctance in democratic America than
in England. To appear on the streets of New York,
about 1800, without a wig was scarcely decent, and
Parton tells us that " many men surrendered the pigtail only with life." In 1786, Ann Warder's Philadelphia nephews wore their hair still in the queue, a
fashion quite gone out at that date in London. She
says: " I threatened the Execusion of these Pig-Tails
before I will submit to introduce them as my nephews
in our country, which they both acknowledge will be
cheerfully resigned." *

In the year 1795, Martha Routh, the English Friend
who wore the first " plain bonnet " in America, attended a meeting of the settlers in the Alleghany
mountains, " to which," she says, " came many Men-
onists and Dunkers. Some of the Elders wear their
beards, as they say, according to ancient custom, but do

---

* Ann Warder, MS. Journal.

not enjoin it as a part of their religion." * These same German Baptists argued that Adam came into being fully equipped with a luxuriant beard; and that Aaron's reached to the hem of his garment. They also quoted Leviticus 19: 27. In respect to Adam, they were hardly behind the Rev. George Wickes, the Puritan divine, who lived during the fashions in dress of the Hogarth period. He died in 1744. A sermon that he preached at Harwichtown has been preserved to us, and is quoted by Bliss. The following extracts seem appropriate:

Adam, so long as he continued in innocency, did wear his own hair and not a Perriwig. Indeed, I do not see how it was possible that Adam should dislike his own hair, and therefore cut it off, so that he might wear a Perriwig, and yet have continued innocent. . . . The children of God will not wear Perriwigs after the Resurrection. . . . Elisha did not cover his head with a Perriwig, altho' it was bald. To see the greater part of Men in some congregations wearing Perriwigs is a matter of deep lamentation. For either all these men had a necessity to cut off their Hair, or else not. If they had a necessity to cut off their Hair, then we have reason to take up a lamentation over the sin of our first Parents which hath occasioned so many Persons in one Congregation to be sickly, weakly crazy Persons. Oh, Adam, what hast thou done! †

Elizabeth Drinker was a Quaker lady of the last century, in Philadelphia, to whose keen powers of observation we are greatly indebted for much valuable information. She writes, in 1794: " Two bearded men drank tea here," recording the fact in much the same way that she had noted the passing by of an elephant, then a rare sight, a short time before.‡ The Puritan was

---

* Martha Routh, Journal, p. 139.

† W. R. Bliss, " Side Glimpses from the Colonial Meeting-house," p. 142.

‡ Elizabeth Drinker, Journal.

everywhere more numerous than the Quaker; and for this reason, his peculiarities occupy a more conspicuous place in literature than those of the latter. His long hair has been noted by no less a hand than that of Ben Jonson. Brother Zeal-of-the-Land Busy, the Puritan in " Bartholomew Fair," is made by the dramatist to say:

For long hair, it is an ensign of Pride, a banner; and the world is full of these banners, very full of banners.*

The famous picture of King Charles I., at St. John's College, Oxford, written in the Psalms, in the smallest possible handwriting that can be deciphered, was thus apostrophized by one Jeremiah Wells:

The Presbyterian maxim holds not here
That calls locks impious if below the ear;
When every fatall clip lops off a prayer,
And he's accurs'd, that dare but cut thy hair.

There are a few rare Quaker pamphlets against wigs. The following extracts from two of the most unique will serve to illustrate the kind of literature devoted to the subject. As usual, in such cases, it is more attractive to the antiquarian than the scholar:

A TESTIMONY AGAINST PERIWIGS AND PERI-WIG MAKING AND PLAYING ON INSTRUMENTS OF MUSIC AMONG CHRISTIANS, OR ANY OTHER IN THE DAYS OF THE GOSPEL. BEING SEVERAL REASONS AGAINST THOSE THINGS. BY ONE WHO FOR GOOD CONSCIENCE SAKE HATH DENYED AND FORSAKEN THEM.
                                   JOHN MULLINER. 1677.

This curious pamphlet relates the suffering of mind undergone by Mulliner, who was at one time a barber of Northampton, in regard to making " borders," wigs and periwigs for his trade. He says:

As to my Employment of Periwig making, it is more than twelve years since I began to make them, and much might be

---

* Act III., Sc. 1.

said for the making of them by some, yet much questioning and reasoning have I had within myself for some time—so that at some times I have been troubled when I have been making of them.

He had apparently argued to himself:

There is hardly any man but is desirous of a good head of Hair, and if Nature doth not afford it, if there be an art to make a Decent Wig or Border, what harm is that? As for those whose hair is wasted, fallen and gone off their Heads through infirmity of Body, and for want of it do find that their health is impaired, or lessened, if such do wear short Borders for their health sake, and for no other End or Cause Whatsoever, I judge them not; but let none make a pretense that they wear Borders or Wigs for their Health, when in Reality, another thing is the Cause.

. . . .

And let all those who have Hair growing upon their heads, sufficient to serve them, I mean what is really needful or useful, be content therewith, and not find fault with their own hair and cut it off, and lust after and put on others Hair.

. . . .

As I had been a publick Professor of this Employment for some time, I must bear my Testimony against them; and that was, I should send for my two men, as I had instructed in that way, and tell them how I was troubled and take a Wig and burn it before them, as a Testimony for God against them. . . . So, according to the pain and sorrow that lay hard upon me, I gave up to do it, and I thank God I have much ease and comfort of mind since I have done it.

. . . .

I was a great lover of Musick, and many times as I have been thinking of God and of the condition I was in, it would have brought trouble upon me; so that many times I have took my Cittern or Treble Viol or any instrument as I had most delight in, thinking to drive away these Thoughts, and I have been so troubled, as I have been playing, that I have laid my instrument down and have reasoned with myself, . . . and fell a crying to God, and my music began to be a burden. . . . I would fain have sold my Instruments, but that I had not freedom in my mind to do; for if I did, those who bought them would have made use of them as I did, and I thought I could not be the cause of it; so

I took as many as I suppose cost forty shilling, and *Burned Them*, and had great Peace in my mind in doing of it, which is more to me than all the pleasures in this world.*

A DECLARATION AGAINST WIGS AND PERIWIGS.
BY RICHARD RICHARDSON.
Jer. 22 : 24. Phil. 3 : 3

Several Testimonies having been given by Friends against Pride in Apparel relating to Women; 'tis considerable whether Women being reflected on, may not reasonably reflect on Men, their artificial frizzled Hair; for Women's Hairs on Men's Heads swarm like one of Egypt's Plagues, and creep in too much upon and among Christians. And a Nehemiah is desirable, that might pluck off this strange Hair of strange Women lusted after. (Nehem. 13: 25.) And the Heathen may rise up against us, for an Ambassador coming before a Senate with false Hair, a Grave Senator said, What credit is to be had to him whose very Locks do lye? And if, upon necessity the Locks of any amongst us do lye, 'tis fit they should lye to purpose, viz., so as not to be discovered from native Locks! For to seek to deceive so as to be perceived, argues as much want of Wit as of Sincerity; and a want of an Endeavor in it not to be perceived, argues a want of Humility and Moderation!

.   .   .   .   .   .

If Heat causes Headach, sure a Wig under a Hat is not a means to cure it. The Prophet Elisha likely had neither, when Bethel Boys cried, A Bald Head!

.   .   .   .   .   .

John Mulliner, A Friend about Northamton, a Wig-maker, left off his trade and was made to burn one in his Prentices sight and Print against it. John Hall, a Gentleman of Northumberland, being Convinced, sitting in a meeting, was shaken by the Lord's Power, pluck'd off and threw down his Wig; so 'tis considerable whether care may not be taken, that conceited conterfit [counterfeit] Calvinists may not continue amongst us, nor that any of the people of God make themselves Bald for Pride now, as they did of old for Sorrow. (Levit. 21. 5.)

.   .   .   .   .   .

The Apostles Peter and Paul forbad ornament of Plaited Hair (as ours translate; Crisp'd or Curl'd, as others) and the An-

---

* This was reprinted in 1708.

cients write, that they both had Bald-Heads, and if they should have covered them with Women's Hair, would they not have retorted Was that the cause, Peter and Paul, that you had us leave off our Locks, that you and such like might get them yourselves to make Peri-wigs of?

And then Friend Richard's feelings overcame him entirely, and he says:

Who can refrain to fall into a Poetical Vein, and Paint out in such sad Colours, that it may look as ugly as it doth. For a glorying in a Shame as an Ornament, Sharppens a Pen to describe it to make it appear as it is. Difficile et Satyram non scribere!

METAMORPHOSES.

The manner of this Age unmannerly
Is, Man unmanning, Women's Hair to buy.
Dub Poles and Joles Dame Venus' knights to be,
Smock-coat and Petticoat-Breech their Livery;
Scarce man-like fac'd, though Woman-like in Hair,
As sting-tail'd Locusts in the Vision were;

.   .   .   .   .   .

And like unto the Phrygian Ganymede,
Or as Tiresias Femaliz'd indeed;
Or one that (sith he would a Woman be)
Put Period to Assyrian Monarchy.
Hair in a Night turn'd Hew, of old 'tis said,
An old man young, a Boy a Girl was made;
Elders so now transform'd to Girls appear,
And Girls to Boys by their short curtail'd Hair.
By bulls, some seem 'ith twilight turn'd to owls,
As antique Harpyes, or some new Night Fowles.
As charming Sirens (bate their ugly Hair)
Having their Arms, Necks, Brests, Backs, Shoulders bare,
Nay, for their Knights rich Garters some prepare.

While long hair was the fashion for men, the collar was unpretending, and an inch or two its utmost height. Henry VIII., who introduced short hair, kept up a simple band of this sort; and no lace was worn. Bands for the neck were of Italian cut-work, costing as

much as £60. "Partelets" were of velvet or lawn,
larger than bands, and worn like the earlier "gorgets"
of embroidered lawn, velvet or Venetian work.*
French gentlemen began to wear collarettes or frilled
ruffles about 1540.† The shirts of this period were of
very fine holland, with no neckband, but a neckcloth,
the most stylish being the "Steenkirk," after the battle of that name. Starch reached the extreme of its use
or abuse in the enormous ruffs of Queen Elizabeth's
reign.‡ Small ruffs were still worn in the early Quaker
times, but they were less starched. Aurelia, in Jasper
Mayne's play, "The City Match," when her Puritan
maid has become worldly, and enters her presence in
fashionable attire, exclaims:

> O, miracle! out of
> Your little ruff, Dorcas, and in the fashion—
> Dost thou hope to be saved? §

and again:

> Ere I'll be tortured thus, I'll get dry palms
> With starching, and put on my smocks myself. ‖

Quarlous, in "Bartholomew Fair," says of an acquaintance:

> Ay, there was a blue-starch woman of the name;

and Nightingale, in the same play, sells "A Ballad of
Goose-green starch and the Devil, i.e, a Goodly ballad
against Pride, showing how a Devil appeared to
a lady which was starching her ruff by night." Yellow starch was most in vogue in England. Old Stubbes

---

* Georgiana Hill, "History of English Dress," Vol. I., p. 187.
† Quicherat, "Histoire de Costume en France," p. 175.
‡ One Mrs. Turner introduced yellow starch from France with great
success. By a dreadful irony of fate she was hanged for the murder of
Sir Thomas Overbury in a starched ruff!
§ Act IV., Sc. 3.
‖ Act II., Sc. 1.

scoffs at " the liquor which they call starch, wherein the devil hath willed them to dye their ruffs! " * He says of their " great ruffes and supportasses " :

They haue great and monstrous ruffes, made either of cambrike, holland, lawne, or els of some other the finest cloth that can be got for money, whereof some be a quarter of a yarde deepe, yea, some more, very few lesse, so that they stande a full quarter of a yearde (and more) from their necks hanging ouer their shoulder points in steade of a vaile. But if Æolus with his blasts, or Neptune with his storms, chaunce to hit vpon the crasie barke of their brused ruffes, then they goe flip flap in the winde like ragges that flew abroade lying vpon their shoulders like the dish cloute of a slut. But wot you what? the deuill, as he, in the fulnesse of his malice, first inuented these great ruffes, so hath he now found out also two great pillers to beare vp and maintaine this his kingdome of pride withal (for the deuill is kyng and prince ouer al the children of pride) The one arch or piller, whereby his kyngdome of great ruffes is vnderpropped, is a certaine kind of liquid matter, whiche they call starch, wherein the deuill hath willed them to washe and diue their ruffes well, whiche, beeying drie, will then stande stiff and inflexible about their necks. The other piller is a certaine deuice made of wiers crested for the purpose whipped ouer either with gold thred, siluer, or silke, and this he calleth a supportasse or vnderpropper; this is to bee applied round about their neckes vnder the ruffe, vpon the out side of the bande, to beare vp the whole frame and bodie of the ruffe, from fallying and hangying doune.

Ruffs gradually went out, clergymen and judges being the last to abandon them, and embroidered muslin or lace collars in Van Dyck style came in. These were worn with no coat collar whatever, in order that they might lie flat on the shoulders; and this is the collar of the time of Penn, whose coat, as we have seen, was collarless. His sovereign's coat was ornamented with a deep lace collar, reaching to the point of the shoul-

---

* " Anatomie of Abuses," 1586.

der, under which any collar of cloth had been impossible. Therefore, when William Penn cast off his laces,
he laid bare his collarless state, and it required one
hundred and fifty years to develop the straight coat cut
of his successors.

But the form of neckwear known as " bands " was
no sooner introduced than it commended itself at once
to the Quaker, and was forthwith adopted. Bands are
the only item of civil dress that the clergy still retain
to-day, surviving in the gown and bands of the Presbyterian Church, as those who know Dr. Parkhurst's
familiar figure will recall. Without entering into the
question of its authenticity as a portrait, Sir Peter
Lely's painting of George Fox in bands is rather striking in connection with our present association of that
portion of the costume with the clergy. The Bevan
portrait of Penn shows him in bands, as does that of
Milton at the age of eighteen. The latter wears the
" falling-band." The bands, worn very soon by most
Quakers, gave them another peculiarity among the
fashionable lace and embroidered collars; and the public
was quick to make a hit. An anti-Quaker tract of
1671 * says: " A Quaker is a vessel of Phanaticism
drawn off to the Lees; a common shore [sewer] of
Heresie, into which most extravagant opinions at last
disembogue and enter; the fag end of Reformation
marked with a sullen meagre look and this characteristic ' Thou.' . . . [He] decries superstition, yet idolizes
Garbs and phrases. You may know him by his diminutive *Band* that looks like the forlorn hope of his shirt

---

* " Character of a Quaker in His True and Proper Colors ; or, The
Clownish Hypocrite Anatomized." London, 1671.

crawling out at his collar, for his purity consists only in his dress, and his religion is not to speak like his neighbors."

Bands were worn by the less fashionable, and by literary and professional men, after they ceased to be universally popular. The Dutch were very partial to them; and the portrait of the painter Le Febvre, with his pupil, in the Louvre, shows both in bands.

Walpole, in his "Anecdotes of Painting," thus describes the Quakers:

A long vest and cloke of black or some other grave colour, with a collar of plain linen called a turnover, and a broad band, with the hair closely cropped, distinguished the men of every rank, and the ladies equally excluded lace, jewels and braided locks.

At one time bands had a certain political significance, and on their introduction into Ireland, in 1728, the following "Answer to the Band Ballad, by a Man Milliner," declared:

The town is alarm'd and seems at a stand,
As if both the Pope and the Devil would land
To doom this whole Isle in the shape of a band—
Which nobody can deny, deny; which nobody can deny.

The bands and lace tie following it were succeeded by the white stock; then came the muslin cravat, which was always a favorite with the Quaker, and a graceful dress at all times; to this succeeded the modern rule of the starched shirt collar, almost as uncompromising in some of its forms as anything worn in the days of Queen Elizabeth. Stiff linen bands, or soft cambric ones, were worn by all Puritans. We find four plain bands and three falling ones supplied to each settler of Massachusetts Bay. Sumptuary laws forbade embroidery. The Judges of the Supreme Court wore bands when on the bench until this century. The linen collar, turned down over the doublet, was known as the "falling band."

GABRIEL-MARC-ANTOINE DE GRELLET,
father of Stephen Grellet. 1789.

CHAPTER IV.

THE QUAKERESS.

Mistress Anne Lovely. — "Isn't it monstrously rediculous that they should desire to impose their quaking dress upon me at these years? When I was a child, no matter what they made me wear; but now — "

Betty.—"I would resolve against it, madam; I'd see 'em hanged before I'd put on the pinch'd cap again."

.   .   .   .

Mistress Lovely.—" Are the pinch'd cap and formal hood the emblems of sanctity? Does your virtue consist in your dress, Mrs. Prim?"

Mrs. Centlivre: "A Bold Stroke for a Wife."

When she to silent meeting comes,
    With apron green before her,
She simpers so like muffle plums,
    'Twould make a Jew adore her.

Old Verse.

Gulielma Springett, 1644-1694.

First Wife of William Penn.

From an engraving after the original painting on glass, in possession of descendants of Henry Swan, of Dorking, England.

CHAPTER IV.

ONCONFORMITY has nowhere expressed itself more fully than in Quaker dress. There is unconscious satire in the old Quaker plea that no change has crept into their institutions; in regard to their dress, at least, this is all a mistake. But one creature exists in which no change, which is the other name for growth, has been going on, and that is the fossil. On the contrary, an instance of adaptability in dress on the part of the Quakers is their prompt acceptance of the shawl, which, at its introduction, near Revolutionary times, was at once seized upon as eminently adapted to Quaker needs. Possibly the most notable instance of adherence to a style is that of Mrs. Noah, in the famous toy ark. It will be remembered that she wears high stays, with a very waspish waist, and her petticoats are extended by what are evidently padded hips. The headdress crowning her rather conventional features—so far as she has any lineaments at all—is a most frivolous "Tam o' Shanter,"—or is it a flat hat, rather circumscribed in extent? At any rate, here is a lady who has dressed just the same for several hundred years, and we should weep to see her change now.

It would be very valuable to us to learn what was the exact costume worn by Margaret Fell (afterward Margaret Fox) and her talented and interesting daughters. We only know how her contemporaries dressed, and have a few details of the family wardrobe in those Swarthmoor account books which still exist. That they wore the popular style of dress, without adornments, is altogether likely, for she has left on record her disapproval of anything tending to *uniformity* among the Friends. We shall not be far wrong, I think, if we imagine George Fox's wife in a hood of black wadded silk, a short, full skirt, standing well out from the hips, and held in position by an array of petticoats (for she would never have worn the false hips then in vogue); a kerchief of muslin, over a low bodice, stiff and long in the waist, and laced with many eyelets, its cord of blue or white or black, depending upon whether her gown were red or blue; her shoes heavy, low and square-toed, with heels that may have been another color from the shoe itself, but not the fashionable red, and higher than we should now care to wear upon the street. Her cloak, whose color we dare not speculate upon, was of substantial cloth, with a hood for ornament when not in use, as it often was, particularly in her long journeys on horseback from county to county attending public meetings. She may have called it a " capuchin," for that was the form of cloak then coming into wear. But we are not privileged to possess descriptions of her personal appearance nor of her style of dress, as is the case with both of her distinguished husbands. We learn from one or two references to old letters of ancient worthies, that she was fair and comely, and

Maria Webb says that she had a " beaming countenance," and a " most sweet, harmonious voice." But
with these slight references we are fain to be content.
A few items of clothing touched upon in the family
letters give us our only clue to the style of dress worn
by the women of the Swarthmoor circle. John Rous,
the son-in-law of Margaret Fell Fox, writes her from
London in 1670:

Yesterday, by John Scott, the Preston carrier, I sent a small
box of sugar for present use, directed for Thomas Green. The
hasp was sealed as this letter is, and in it was a white mantle,
and a white sarsanet hood for thee, and some playthings for the
children.*

The following items from a portion of the old
Swarthmoor Account Book of 1673, which is quoted
from at length in " The Fells of Swarthmoor Hall,"
are very interesting for the light they throw upon the
style of dress in the Fell family. The precious old book
is in Sarah Fell's handwriting. Sarah was the eldest
daughter of the household, and the head of affairs and
its business manager, to whom, after her marriage with
William Meade, the whole family, including her
mother, repeatedly appealed in despair to clear up the
confusion into which Swarthmoor affairs immediately
fell after she left the home. In some cases the cost of
the articles given is illegible:

By money pd. Thos. Benson for dying 2 pr. stockings sky colour, of mine, and a petticoat red, of
   mine . ... (Defaced)
By money pd. for a hat for little Mary Lower I
   gave her 0   0   6
For 20 yds. Cumberland cloth 2   0   9
Paid for a vizard mask for myself & a hat ...... (Defaced)

---

* Maria Webb, " The Fells of Swarthmoor Hall," p. 231.

By money pd. for 1 yd. and nail of black paragon for apron for self	0	2	0
Paid for leading strings for little Margaret Lower	0	0	2
By money paid for a blue apron and strings for myself	0	1	3
By money pd. for a black hood for sister Susan....	0	4	0
By money pd. for a black alamode whiske* for sister Rachel	0	2	0
By money paid for a round whiske for sister Susanna	0	4	4
Do. for a little black whiske for myself	0	1	10
1678.			
By money pd. for clogging a pair of clogs and for nailes to mend shoes for my boy, Tom Harrison, (own account)	0	0	5½

Sarah (Fell) Meade wrote to her sister, Rachel Abraham, from London, under date " The 19th. of 10th. [December] 1683 ":

I have endeavoured to fit my dear Mother with black cloth for a gown, which is very good and fine, and as much as Jno. Richards saith is enough to the full, 5 yards and half, and what materials as he thought was needful to send down, vizt. silk, both sewing and stitching, gallowne ribbon, and laces, and I was very glad to know what she wanted, for it has been in my mind a pretty while to send her and you something, and I could not tell what she might need or might be most serviceable to her was the reason of my thus long forbearance, and so I desire her acceptance of it, and yours of the small things underwritten:

3 pair doe skin gloves such as are worn in winter, for mother, sister Lower and thyself; the thickest pair for mother if they fit her, but that I leave to you to agree on as you please.

1 pair same sort of gloves for brother Abraham.

4 ells of Holland, for sister Lower and thyself, each two ells.

2 pots of balsam, one for my mother, the other for sister Yeamans.

3 pocket almanacs, for sister Yeamans, sister Lower and thyself.

---

*Whisk, " A neckerchief worn by women in the seventeenth century. Also called ' falling-whisk,' apparently to distinguish it from the ruff." —" The Century Dictionary."

1 muslin nightrail for sister Yeamans, which she sent for.
100 needles, of which half for sister Yeamans, which she sent
for, the other half hundred for sister Lower and thyself.

. . . . . .

There is (in the box) for sister Lower, which she sent to sister
Susanna to buy her, a colored stuff manteo, cost 14s., and 11
yards and half of black worsted stuff, at 2s. per yard, cost 22s.
Sister Susanna exchanged the old 20s. piece of gold as she desired,
which yielded 23s. 6d., so she is out of purse for her 12s. 6d.
Black stuff was worse to get than colored, which is now mostly
worn; but she hath done as well as she can, and hopes it will
please her; its a strong, serviceable stuff.

. . . . . .

Mary Frith presents her service to (sister Yeamans), and
takes it kindly that she should send her her fillet.

. . . . . .
                    I am thy affectionate sister,   S. M.
(P. S.)
    We advise you to make my mother's cloth gown without a
skirt, which is very civil, and usually so worn, both by young
and old, in stiffened suits.*

These were all women of cultivation and good taste,
and the sister in London kept them posted as to the
correct mode of dress, with an evident desire that their
mother should not be allowed to appear singular in her
garb, although no time was wasted by any of them on
the frivolities of dress. The simple, homely view
of the family life presented in these and other letters of the Fells, allows us to clothe them with a personality that gives them a living charm when we meet
them again in the larger arena of public life, in court or
prison. Making " my mother's gown without a skirt "
is probably making it without an overdress of any
sort, the full, stiffened petticoats that were then the
mode requiring none. The Quaker women had been

---

*Maria Webb, "The Fells of Swarthmoor Hall," p. 92.

wearing the short overskirt represented in the Quakeress Tub-Preacher,* and it was evidently to this that the reference was made. The " whisk " above referred to is the forerunner of the handkerchief worn by Elizabeth Fry and her successors ever since.

Sometimes the modest dress of the Quakers was sadly misrepresented, and when the course of true love in the case of Thomas Lower and Mary, daughter of Judge Fell and Margaret (afterward Fox), did not at first run quite smoothly, certain persons at Plymouth circulated a description of her and her sister that Thomas hastened to deny. He writes Mary:

At Plymouth both thou and sister Yeamans were painted with naked necks, and in costly array, until T. S. [Thomas Salthouse] and I deciphered you, and quite defaced the former counterfeit by representing you in a more commendable dress. The authors of these unsavory belchings I cannot fully discover, but that which brings report will also carry.

The Fells lived in days of more extravagance of taste than we, although a recent writer on modern dress asserts that women to-day appear " one season like wriggling worms in lampshades, and the next, festooned and befringed in the upholstery of a four-post bedstead." †

No wonder that Fox, to whom it must have been as gall and wormwood to be obliged to touch upon the subject at all, cried out, in a moment of wrath and indignation, to the women of his day, " Away with your long slit peaks behind in the skirts of your waistcoats," " your skimming-dish hats," " unnecessary buttons,"

* See illustration, " The Quaker Meeting."
† Lady Gwendolen Ramsden, " The Nineteenth Century," for November, 1900, " On Extravagance in Dress."

"short sleeves," "short black aprons," "vizzards," "your great needless flying scarfs, like colours [flags] on your backs." But they went on, the world's people; and the Quakers of Queen Anne's time saw fashions come and go that beside the beautiful costumes of the great days of Van Dyck and Bol, seem the very embodiment of grotesqueness—the hoop, the periwig, and the tight stays. Finally, in 1770, an Act was passed by Parliament to the effect that

All women, of whatever age, rank, profession, degree, whether virgins, maids or widows, that shall from and after such Act impose upon seduce or betray into matrimony, any of his Majesty's male subjects by the scents, paints, cosmetics, washes, artificial teeth, false hair, Spanish wool, iron-stays, hoops, high-heeled shoes, etc., shall incur the penalty of the law now in force against *witchcraft*, and like misdemeanors, and that the marriage upon conviction shall be null and void!*

Of the two wives of William Penn we possess a fine portrait of the first—the fair Gulielma Springett, whose life and love are one of the sweet romances of Quakerism. She is represented in the silk hood worn by the mother and the wife of Cromwell, and by most of the nobility and gentry of England in her day, with the border of a dainty muslin cap showing beneath. Her brocaded gown is short and very full at the hips; the pointed laced bodice cut low in the neck, and filled in with a kerchief; the elbow sleeves turned back in a large loose cuff, beneath which fine muslin under-sleeves appear. It is probable that her dress does not represent the costume of the plainest Friends of her day, any more than did that of her distinguished husband. But the dress of contemporary modish ladies

---

* Georgiana Hill, " Women in English Life," Vol. I., p. 317.

with which we are able to compare it is so vastly more elaborate than " Guli's," that we at once recognize the presence of Quaker moderation, combined with taste and good sense, such as we should expect in the daughter of Lady Springett. Hannah Callowhill, the second wife of William Penn, brought up in the rather austere community of Friends in Bristol, whose mercantile atmosphere did not foster the arts or the graces of life among her immediate family or associates, represents an older woman, in sober attire, whose gowns and aprons were of a plainer hue, and whose whole mien was one of seriousness and sobriety. The portrait that we have of her is also taken in the hood, and there is no evidence of any cap underneath.*

The Quakeresses were not unfamiliar in their modest garb to the lords and ladies about the Court. Seven of them, in 1765, went together to wait upon Queen Charlotte, " when her Majesty ordered her lady-in-waiting to compliment each of them, which they returned in a sensible and modest manner." † Margaret Fell, both before and after her marriage to George Fox, made various visits to the Court, usually accompanied by another woman Friend.

Aberdeen and Dublin seem to have been from the

---

* The original of the portrait of Gulielma Penn is a painting on glass in the possession of the descendants of Henry Swan, of Holmwood, Dorking, England, who died in 1796. The copy from which this present example is taken, forms the frontispiece to the " Penns and Penningtons of the Seventeenth Century," by Maria Webb.

The portrait of Hannah Penn is from a painting in the Banqueting Room of Independence Hall, Philadelphia. This is a copy in its turn of a crayon drawing in possession of a descendant of Francis Place, the artist, who lived near Darlington. Place is said to have taken the portrait during one of the frequent visits of the Penns to their sister, who lived near him.

† British Museum " Scrap Book " (4152, H, 5).

Hannah   Callowhill, 1664-1726.

Second Wife of William Penn.

Original painting at Blackwell Hall, County Durham, England.
Copy in Independence Hall, Philadelphia.

I.

II.

The Collar.

I. Miss Fitzgerald, Lady-in-Waiting to Queen Caroline, 1800.
After the painting by Sir Thomas Lawrence.

II. Margaret Morris, Wife of Isaac Collins, Jr., 1792-1832.
From the drawing on stone of A. Newsam, after
the original painting.

first the meetings most anxious to keep their membership as plain as possible. The former issued an early
" Testimony " to the effect that " no colored plaids be
worn any more, but either mantles or low hoods." An
order prohibiting plaids, in the land of the Scotch, did
violence to long-cherished traditions of patriotism and
clan-feeling, and the Aberdeen Friends wasted many
years in trying to enforce arbitrary laws of dress. The
Friends give gaiety as the ground of their objection to
plaids, and herein show their want of tact, for this garment had fallen under condemnation for another reason
than its fashion among the Scotch in the town of Glasgow, where the Kirk Session Books say: * " Great dis-
order hath been in the Kirk by reason of women sitting
with their heads covered in time of sermon, sleeping."
This led to condemnation of hoods, under whose
friendly protection the Scotch women could indulge in
a refreshing nap during the interminable sermons of the
Scotch clergy. Thirty years later, in 1637, the plaids
worn by the plain folk over the head were condemned
for the same reason, and not, as has been thought, for
the gay coloring.

The clothing of the common people, as well as of the
more well-to-do, was spun by the women of the family,
and woven by the village " wabster." The spinning-
wheel was in use in England in the time of the first
Friends, but in many of the country districts, and
almost everywhere in Scotland, the old " rock and
reel " were still employed. The " rock " was the hand
distaff, referred to by Spenser in the " Faery Queen "
(IV., iii. 48):

* Planché, " Dictionnaire de Costume," p. 244.

Sad Clotho held the rocke, the whiles the thrid
By griesly Lachesis was spun with paine.

Burns also makes Bess, in "Bess and her Spinning-Wheel," say:

Oh, leeze me on my spinning wheel,
Oh, leeze me on my rock and reel.

1730 saw the wheel introduced into Scotland, before which " rockings," somewhat corresponding to our old quilting parties, were great social events. The cloth thus prepared was made up into garments at home, or by traveling tailors, for a milliner was only known in the large cities, where her business was not only to clothe the living, but to " dress dead corpses," and sell " dead flannels." The peripatetic tailor was paid two or three pence a day and his food, or " diet." The traveling weaver was also an institution, and bought the thrifty housewife's yarn, giving or selling in exchange new and tempting webs of cloth. The " dead flannels " referred to were the wool garments in which, according to the law of England, in 1678, enacted in order to encourage the wool trade, all corpses were required to be buried, heavy fines being imposed for its evasion. Friends were usually careful to comply with these requirements, as instances on record in minutes of various meetings abundantly show.

Many of the first Quaker women were of the peasant class, as would be natural with the converts of a race of open air preachers. A very short time saw ladies of wealth and position, like Lady Springett, taking their places in the meetings; but the women of the fields were wearers of homespun gowns, and not until the next century were these confined to any special color. Red was very popular in the early half of the seventeenth century; and scarlet was common among the Quaker women, as it always has been among the peasants of other countries besides England, both for its apparent warmth, and for its lasting qualities. Among the household accounts of Margaret Fell we find charges for scarlet cloth, after the manner of the good housekeeper in the Book of Proverbs, who " clothed her household in scarlet." When she became the wife of George Fox he bought her scarlet cloth for a mantle. He writes his wife, about 1678, that with the money she had sent him to buy clothes for himself he purchased of Richard Smith a piece of " red cloth for a mantle, believing she needed that more than he needed the coat." Again, from Worcester prison, he wrote to her that he had got a friend to purchase " as much black Spanish cloth as would make her a gown," with what she had given him, adding, " It cost a great deal of money, but I will save." *

It is to be hoped that she did not wear with her gay wrap one of the green aprons that the Friends were then regarding as almost the badge of Quakerism, and which were so identified with the Quaker women that the satires then plentiful in the shape of broadsides and pamphlets, all made playful allusions to the green aprons.

This garment happened to be in high favor at the time the Quakers arose, and to this accident is due many an entry in minutes of Dublin, Aberdeen and London meetings, advising their young women with great detail as to the style and color of their aprons. The fashion

---

* Maria Webb, " The Fells of Swarthmoor Hall," p. 259.

held for many years, and this important article of costume was worn by court lady and little scullery maid
alike. The favorite color with everybody was green
at first; long afterward we find Swift writing to
Stella:

You shall have your aprons; and I'll put all your commissions
as they come in a paper together; and don't think I'll forget
(your) orders because they are friend's; I'll be as careful as if
they were stranger's.*

The apron is described as of green silk, in a letter of
April 24th. Later (October 30th, 1711):

Who'll pay me for this green apron? I will have the money,
it cost ten shillings and six pence. I think it plaguey dear for
a cheap thing, but they said that English silk would cockle, and
I know not what.

In the following year Swift has several more commissions from Stella for green aprons from the metropolis.

In 1698, Aberdeen Meeting said:

Let none want aprons at all, and that either green or blue,
or other grave colors, and not white upon the street or in public at all, nor any spangled or speckled silk or cloth or any silk
aprons at all. And dear Friends, we being persuaded that none
of a right spirit will be so stiff or so willful as to prefer their
own lusts or wills to our tender sense or advice, and labor of
love in these things.†

The Women's Quarterly Meeting of Lincolnshire,
21st of Fourth month, 1721, says:

We think green aprons are very decent and becoming us as a
people.

In 1735, a young woman Friend named May Drummond, of Edinburgh, who appears to have been a per-

---

* Journal to Stella, April 5th, 1711.
† Aberdeen, " A Testimony," 5 mo. 28th, 1698.

son of attractive appearance, and much real ability, was
given an audience with Queen Caroline. An original
letter of that date, from which the following is an extract, gives an interesting description of her ministry
and personal appearance, and emphasizes the green
apron. She is described as preaching to audiences of
more than three thousand people. The writer then goes
on:

> She hath also been to wait on the Queen, and was more than
> an hour in her presence. Att her first coming in the Queen soon
> began and asked her many questions which May was not very
> forward to answer, but after some little pawce she began and had
> a good opportunity for near half an hour (with little interrup-
> tion) To speake to the Queen the Princesses and some Ladys
> of honour (so called) which she and those three friends who
> accompanied her had good reason to think was very much to all
> their satisfaction ffor she spoke in such a tender handsome and
> moving manner that pretty much affected all present so that I
> believe that her visit was not onely acceptable but of very good
> service. The Queen seemed much pleased with her plain dress, and
> *green apron,* and often said she thought it exceedingly neat and
> becoming.

The French country women in the reign of Louis
XI. wore white aprons at work, or in demi-toilette,
when going to the town to market. The negligée of 1672
consisted of a black dress with a white apron, and we
are told by Boursault (" Mots à la Mode ") the name of
this apron:

> L'homme le plus grossier et l'esprit le plus lourd,
> Sait qu'un " Laisse-tout-faire " est un tablier court.

After the regency the apron, having had a period of
disfavor, reappeared in France on young people, and
was a part of ordinary costume, the overdress 'being
abandoned and the apron worn with a jacket ("caraco")
and a flounced skirt. The apron descended to the bor-

der of the gown, had pockets, and was trimmed on the edge. It was without ends ("bavettes"), a style confined to chambermaids.* Miss Hill describes a lady of Queen Anne's day thus:

She wore a black silk petticoat with red and white calico border, cherry-colored stays, trimmed with blue and silver, red and dove-colored damask gown flowered with large trees, a yellow satin apron trimmed with white Persian, muslin head-cloth with crowfoot edging, double ruffles with fine edging, a black silk fur-belowed scarf and a spotted hood! †

A bride in the middle of the eighteenth century wore a sprigged muslin apron trimmed with lace, over a silver muslin "night-gown"—(an elegant affair, probably so called because *not* worn at night). Nollekin's wife also wore on her wedding day "an elegant lace apron." The opening of the nineteenth century saw the Parisians adoring simplicity, and they took back into favor again the discarded white apron, which soon became a part of full dress. The rustic straw hat à la shepherdess was in favor as also in England, and the gipsy hat tied down with a ribbon or a silk handkerchief. Straw was worn only with morning dress; the time of year mattered little.

During the latter half of the eighteenth century the plainest women among the Friends wore aprons of what now seem very gay colors—blue, green, etc. The reason for this is that the white apron was in the height of fashion. Watson, the Annalist, says, in writing of a period about 1770:

The plainest women among the Friends (now so averse to fancy colours), wore their coloured silk aprons, say of green or blue,

---

* Quicherat, "Histoire de Costume en France," pp. 328, 520, 574.
† Georgiana Hill, "History of English Dress," Vol. II., p. 73.

etc. This was at a time when the "gay" wore white aprons. In time, white aprons were disused (by the latter), and then the Friends left off their colored ones and used white.

A letter of Richard Shackleton's * dated Ballitore, 14th Third month, 1776, shows that the green apron, even, had its dangers, in its tendency to become a special costume for wear on occasions of public meetings, or during the time of religious worship:

What shall I say about these green aprons? I think we are of one mind about them. I believe it is the Master's mind that His disciples and followers should be distinguished from the world by a singularity of external appearance. I suppose it is also His will that a certain peculiarity of habit should distinguish them on the solemn occasion of assembling for Divine worship, or other religious performances.

When Sarah, the wife of George Dillwyn, was in London, in 1784, she wrote to a member of her family:

I think the women here far before the men—they dress extremely neat and exact, a few of the plainest with black hoods and green aprons. Some go to meeting without aprons, but generally carry fine muslin or cambric ones in their pockets, to put on when they get in the house; if we don't bring one, they always offer.

This also shows us the time of transition from the green to the white apron, which did not lose its hold among the plainer Quakeresses for nearly a hundred years.

The skirt of the dress was worn with very full gathers, soon followed by false hips, and the natural successor to this was of course the famous hooped petticoat of history and song, which made its appearance in 1709. The crinoline, or hoop, was invented by one Mrs. Selby, remaining through a longer period than the

---

* Quoted by R. Morris Smith, "The Burlington Smiths," p. 157.

old farthingale, and was eventually banished by George IV.* The following appeared at Bath in 1711:

THE FARTHINGALE REVIVED: OR MORE WORK FOR THE COOPER. A PANEGYRICK ON THE LATE, BUT MOST ADMIRABLE INVENTION OF THE HOOPED PETTICOAT.

There's scarce a bard that writ in former time
Had e'er so great, so bright a theme for rhyme.
The Mantua swain, if living, would confess
Ours more surprising than his Tyrian dress;
And Ovid's mistress, in her loose attire,
Would cease to charm his eyes, or fan Love's fire.
Were he in Bath, and had these coats in view,
He'd write his metamorphosis anew.
Delia, fresh hooped, would o'er his heart prevail
To leave Corinna and her tawdry veil.

1835.

The hoop-petticoat was, no doubt, thought very fine in the country. It had the merit, which many fashions did not possess, of bestowing importance upon the wearer. "Insignificant-looking women, to whom before nobody had paid any attention, now came into notice; and portly women became positively awful in their majesty!" †

The style had a great revival 1850-1865, both with gay and plain.

---

* The stomacher was an earlier garment, introduced in the fifteenth century. It was worn by both sexes, and by King Edward IV.

† A POPULAR BALLAD OF 1733.

What a fine thing have I seen to-day,
    Oh Mother, a hoop!
I must have one, you cannot say nay—
    Oh Mother, a hoop!
For husbands are gotten this way, to be sure,
Men's eyes and Men's hearts they so neatly allure.
    Oh Mother, a hoop, a hoop; Oh Mother, a hoop!
                                —Percy Soc., Vol. xxvii., p. 220.

There are no doubt to be found in the archives of many old Quaker families certain queer and very ugly long jackets of a shapeless sort of pattern, known in their day and generation as a " short-gown." The " short-gown and petticoat " may be met with in literature occasionally still, or in the letters of our great-grandmothers. It is difficult to understand the early enthusiasms over such a thoroughly inartistic garment; perhaps feminine ingenuity found an outlet in its decoration rather than its outline. At all events, the muse became thus inspired:

THE SHORT-BODY'D GOWN. (1801.)

Last midsummer day Sally went to the fair,
For to sell her yarn. Oh, how she did stare!
Both wives, maids and widows, in every shop round,
They all were dressed up in a short-body'd gown!

So home in the evening Miss Sally she hies,
And tells it her mother with greatest surprise;
Saying, " Two hanks a day will I spin the week round
Until I can purchase a short-body'd gown.*

When Ann Warder landed in New York, in 1786, she wrote to her sister in London:

The women all wear short gowns, a custom so truly ugly that I am mistaken if I ever fall into it. Notwithstanding they say I shall soon be glad to do it on account of the heat.

Thomas Chalkley was sufficiently moved by the horrors of the hoop to say:

If Almighty God should make a woman in the same shape her hoop makes her, Everybody would say truly it was monstrous. So according to this real truth they make themselves monstrous by art.

---

* Percy Society, Vol. XXVII., p. 264.

The bodices worn at the time that dress begins to be a subject for official notice in meetings were laced, and opened in front, exposing the tight stays in gay colors worn beneath them. The bodice was cut very low, the

bosom being covered with a "tucker" or "modesty piece" worn across the top of the bodice in front. In 1713 we find the *Guardian* growling at the ladies who are beginning to discard the latter in order to follow the fashion. The year 1800 finds the court ladies wearing a becoming broad muslin collar of very "sheer" quality, and the Quakeresses adopted the style quite

1787.

generally, as may be seen by comparing the two illustrations of that date. In 1644, when gowns were very décolleté, Quicherat tells us that the ladies wore, en negligée, a white fichu or handkerchief, known as the "whisk," and a linen or fine lace scarf for dress. This simplicity was encouraged by Anne of Austria. The handkerchief seems to have been the one portion of the Quakeress dress that has come down unchanged to modern times.

Thus it was with the "world's people," and as Quaker persecution ceased, vanity in dress arose, alas! even among them; poor Susan Ponder was disowned for "conforming to the fashions of this wicked world." Aberdeen Meeting has an elaborate description of what is and is not to be suffered in men's and women's dress. In 1703 the young women came to York Quarterly Meeting in long cloaks and the new Paris importation called the " bonnet." They were therefore not only ordered to take the advice of their elders before coming to " these great meetings here in York," but one subordinate meeting actually ordered the young women of its own meeting to appear before it "in those clothes that they intend to have on at York." * However, neither this, nor the strict oversight of Aberdeen, was sufficient in the early years to exclude all worldliness; for in 1720 we find all these vanities noted in the minutes of the latter as existing among the young Quakeresses: " Quilted petticoats, set out in imitation of hoops; cloth shoes of a light color, with heels white and red; scarlet and purple stockings, and petticoats made short to expose them." In that year, York Quarterly Meeting sent the following letter to the monthly meetings composing its constituency, which was in its turn sent to each particular meeting of women. The original from which this is copied was directed to " the Women Friends of Rilston Meeting, These." †

Att our Quarterly Meeting held att York, ye 22 & 23 4th. Mon. 1720 The Monthly Meets. were called & there was thatt answered for all, either by Representatives or papers & most gave account thatt things were pretty well amongst them notwithstanding there are severall things remains amongst us wch are very Burthensome to the honest-hearted & have been weightily spoken against wch its Desired the Representatives would Deliver in the Wisdom of Truth (viz.) the imitating the Fashions of the World in their Headclothes some haveing four pinner ends hang-

---

* Robert Barclay, " Inner Life of the Religious Societies of the Commonwealth," p. 491.

† Devonshire House Collection, London.

ing Down* and handkerchiefs being too thin some haveing them
hollowed out & putt on farr of their necks also their gown
sleeves & short capps wth a great Deal to pinn up in the Skirt
also their Quilted petticoats sett out in imitation of hoops some
wearing two together also cloth Shoes of light Colors bound wth
Differing colours and heels White or Red wth White Bands and
fine Coloured Clogs & strings also Scarlet or Purple Stockings &
petticoats made Short to Expose ym. Friends are also Desired to
keep out of the fashion of wearing black hats or shaving
[chip] or straw ones with crowns too little or two large wth
wch else the Judgment of Truth is gone out agst.

Signed in behalf of the meeting by

>   MARY WHITE,
>   SARAH ELAM,
>   HANNAH ARMITSTEAD,
>   TAMER FIELDING,
>   MARY SLATER.

The early Quaker women wore their hair, like that
of the men, cut low and straight on the forehead, and
braided or put in a knot on the top of the head. It
was the era when the great commode was approaching,
reaching its height in the reign of Queen Anne. This
perilous structure consisted of " a frame of wire two or
three stories high, fitted to the head and covered with
tiffany or rather thin silk now completed into a headdress." †   The word " commode " was never used for
this head dress in America.

>   Nor holy church is safe, they say,
>   Where decent veil was wont to hide
>   The modest sex' religious pride;
>   Lest these yet prove too great a load,

---

* Pinners appear to have been the pendant ends, streamers, or lappets, hanging down at the sides of the face, or occasionally behind—like
" liripipes," which were longer, and always at the back. These were
all quite distinct from cap *strings*.

† " The Book of Costume. By a Lady of Quality." London, 1846.

'Tis all compris'd in the commode;
Pins tipt with diamond, point and head,
By which the curls are fastened,
In radiant firmament set out,
And over all the hood sur-tout.
Thus, face that e'rst near head was plac'd
Imagine now about the wast,
For tour on tour, and tire on tire,
Like steeple Bow, or Grantham spire,
Or Septizonium, once at Rome,
(But does not half so well become
Fair ladies' head) you here behold
Beauty by tyrant mode controll'd.*

The articles required in a lady's toilet bore many
and curious names; they were so incomprehensible to
the uninitiated, that the following anecdote is most
amusing:

A raw lass, being entertained in service, and hearing her mistress one day call for some of them, she was so far from bringing any, that she verily took her to be conjuring, and hastily ran
out of the house, for fear she should raise the devil! †

The contrast to the Quakeress may be imagined. A
French style in favor at this time also consisted of a
bandeau of jewels worn over flowing locks in negligent
fashion on the shoulders, to match the " love-lock " of
the men. The " love-lock " was introduced by Charles
I., and consisted of a curl of greater length than the
rest of the hair, worn on the left side. This soon became the rage. A corresponding lock with the ladies

---

*From "Mundus Mulieribus, or, The Ladies Dressing-Room
unlocked, and Her Toilet spread," 1670. Anonymous. This is an elaborate description of women's costume. It is given in the publications of
the Percy Society. Vol. XXVII., p. 190.

†Quoted by Repton, "Archæologia." Vol. XXVII., p. 56.

was the " heart-breaker." * The high headdress lasted much later than the love-lock. In 1698 we find Jonathan Edwards rebuking its appearance in Puritan New England. The Puritan women are often represented with " banged " hair. The " high head " had a period of decadence, and was revived again in 1715, and Addison writes soon after: " There is not so variable a thing in nature as a Lady's headdress; within my memory I have known it rise and fall above thirty degrees." " I pretend not to draw the quill against that immense crop of plumes." The " commode " killed itself by its own extravagance, the time and expense required to put up one's hair becoming so great that the hair-dresser could not make his rounds to any but the most wealthy oftener than once in three weeks or a month, leading one satirical writer of the period to remark:

I consent also to the present style of curling the hair so that it may stay a month without combing, tho' I must confess that I think 3 weeks or a fortnight might be sufficient time!

The tremendous " crop," or turban, that all lovers of " Cranford " will remember, was a favorite of the ladies later on. The moment a woman became a Quaker, the fact was proclaimed to all the world by her discarding all extravagant headdresses. The early Methodists were quite as pronounced. An old Norfolk journal has the following:

Several fine ladies who used to wear French silks, French hoops, 4 yards wide, tête de mouton heads, and white satin smock petticoats, are now turned Methodists, and followers of

---

* Another "heart-breaker" is described as "False Locks set on Wyers to make them stand at a distance," about 1670. They resembled butterfly wings over the ears.

Mr. Whitefield, whose doctrine of the new birth has so prevailed over them, that they now wear plain stuff gowns, no hoops, common night mobs, and old plain bags!

Stubbes, from whom we have before quoted, describes the elaborate coiffure of an elegant dame:

Then followeth the trimming and tricking of their heades, in laying out their haire to the shewe, whiche of force must be curled, fristed, and crisped, laid out (a world to see) on wreathes and borders, from one eare to another. And least it should fall down, it is vnder propped with forks, wiers, and I cannot tell what, like grim sterne monsters, rather than chaste Christian matrones. Then on the edges of their boulstered hair (for it standeth crested rounde their frontiers, and hanging ouer their faces like pendices or uailes, with glasse windowes on euery side) there is laide great wreathes of golde and siluer curiously wrought, and cunningly applied to the temples of their heades. And for feare of lacking anything to set forthe their pride withall, at their haire, thus wreathed and creasted, are hanged bugles (I dare not say bables), ouches, ringes, gold, siluer, glasses, and suche other childish gewgaws, and foolish trinkets besides, whiche, for they are innumerable, and I vnskilfull in women's termes I cannot easily expresse. But God giue them grace to giue ouer their vanities, and studie to adorn their heades with the incorruptible ornaments of vertue and true godlinesse.

The ancient London graveyard of the Friends, in Lower Redcross Street, Southwark, was removed a few years since, not having had any interment made in it since 1799. One of the graves was found to be that of a young woman who wore on her head a pad quite perfect, such as was customary at the time to keep the hair high on the crown; and in the mass of auburn hair, long and fine, was a handsome tortoise shell comb.* This would indicate the tendency, before alluded to, for the Quakers to follow the dictates of fashion, even at a safe distance. It was a passing fancy in the early

* Beck and Ball, "The London Friends' Meetings," p. 238.

days to draw up the petticoat through the pocket hole
and other openings, thereby displaying the gaiety of
that garment. We may note the case of the maid,
who being required by John Bolton, on an order from
George Fox, to sew up the slit in her waist-coat skirt
behind, answered that she " saw no evil in it; and
James Claypoole thought it suitable to their principle
that she should first see the evil in it herself before she
judged it, and not (saith he) because we say it." *
Wherein James showed great discrimination. The
Quakeresses who wore the hair low were really more
in the French mode, the artistic sense of that nation
rebelling sooner against the rule of the " commode,"
which seems after the law of contraries to have won its
name from its inconvenience, much as the " night-
gown " and " night-cap " were elegant constructions,
never worn at night!

February 15th, 1765, the Duchess of Devonshire
wrote to her mother:

> I was too tired to write. My sister and I were very smart for
> Carlton House. Our gowns were night-gowns of my invention.
> The body and sleeves black velvet bound with pink, and the
> skirt, apron and handkerchie crape, bound with light pink, and
> large chip hats with feathers and pinks. My sister looked vastly
> pretty.

Of course all the Germans of the last century were
devotees of the " schlafrock," which, however, was
emphatically a lounging garment, a purpose with
which is instinctively associated all our ideas of the
old-time German " Herr Professor," who never made
his toilet until the working hours of the day were

---

* " Tyranny and Hypocrisy Detected." — Answer to a pamphlet,
" The Spirit of the Hat." London, 1673.

over, and not always then. Macbeth dons a "night-gown," and so does Julius Cæsar, both being loose robes.

Henrietta Maria, Queen of Charles I., in her well-known portrait in the National Gallery, wears her hair curled, and is seen in a simple yellow satin gown, with broad lace at the low neck, and at the elbow sleeves. She wears a pearl necklace and chain. Catherine, Duchess of Queensbury (1700-1777), the daughter of Lord Clarendon, and the patroness of Gay, Prior and others, called by Walpole, "Prior's Kitty, ever young," wears in her portrait in the National Gallery a costume almost Quaker-like in its simplicity, with a simple coiffure, and a kerchief thrown over the shoulders. Even Nell Gwynn (1650-1687) is simple in short sleeves, low neck, and short curly hair.

1756.

Thomas Story, whose wide acquaintance took him among the "world's people," tells us of an attempt he made to convert the Countess of Kildare to Quaker dress:

It being the Time of the Assizes, many of the higher Rank were in Town on that Occasion, and divers of our Friends being acquainted with several of them, one Day came to my Friend John Pike's to Dinner, the young Countess of Kildare, and her Maiden Sister, and three more of lesser Quality of the Gentry. Upon this occasion we had some free and open Conversation together, in which this Lady and the rest commended the plain Dress of our Women, as the most decent and comely, wishing it were in Fashion among them. Upon this I told her "That she and the rest of her Quality, standing in Places of Eminence, were the fittest to begin it, especially as they saw a Beauty in it; and they would be sooner followed than those of lower Degree." To this she replied, "If we should Dress ourselves Plain, People would gaze at us, call us Quakers, and make us the Subject of their Discourse and Town-talk; and we cannot bear to be made so particular."

I answered, "The Cause is so good, being that of Truth and Virtue, if you will espouse it heartily upon its just Foundation, a few of you would dash out of Countenance, with a steady and fixed Gravity, Abundance of the other Side, who have no Bottom but the Vain Customs of The Times; and you will find a Satisfaction in it, an Overbalance to all you can lose, since the Works of Virtue and Modesty carry in them an immediate and perpetual Reward to the Worker." This seemed not unpleasant, being said in an open Freedom; But then, alas! all was quenched at last by this; they all of them alledged, "That our own young Women of any Note, about London and Bristol, went as fine as they with the finest of Silk and Laced Shoes; and when they went to Bath, made as great a Show as any." Not knowing but some Particulars might give too much occasion for this Allegation, it was a little quenching; but, with some Presence of Mind, I replied, "I have been lately at London and Bristol, and also at the Bath, and have not observed any such; but at all these three Places generally indifferent plain, and many of them, even of the younger sort, very well on that Account; But such among us who take such Liberties, go beside their Profession, and are no Examples of Virtue, but a dishonour and Reproach to our Profession, and a daily and perpetual Exercise to us; and I hope you will not look at the Worst, since, among us everywhere, you may find better and more general Examples of Virtue and Plainness." This they did not deny; and so that Part ended.*

London Quarterly Meeting, in 1717, issued a paper in which the women are exhorted not to deck themselves with " gaudy and costly apparel," nor to wear " gold chains, lockets, necklaces and gold watches exposed to open view." The " immodest fashion of hooped petticoats " is condemned; the wearing of mourning, and worldly conversation. " Likewise there is a declension crept in among us of unbecoming ges-

---

* Thomas Story, Journal. Folio edition, p. 533. 1716.

tures in cringing and bowing of the body by way of salutation, which ought not to be taught or countenanced in our schools or families." The document then asks:

How shall any persons reputed Quakers wearing extravagant wigs, open breasts, their hats and clothes after a beauish fashion, gold chains with lockets and gold watches openly exposed, like the lofty dames, or hooped petticoats, like the wanton women, be distinguished from the loose, proud people of the world?*

Stubbes had declared † that the perfumes so prevalent at this time were " engines of pride, allurements to sinne, and provocations to vice ! " If cleanliness is next to godliness, old Stubbes may indeed have been right; for the heavy odors in use covered up a multitude of sins. The prevalent use of snuff made the silk handkerchief a necessity. A few dainty folk used those of cambric. An old advertisement calls attention to " handkerchiefs that will wash in a weak lather of soap without prejudice." ‡ The custom of ladies smoking was a fad with the " smart set " of that day as well as our own. They still painted, a custom which Evelyn (11th of May, 1654) had noticed beginning: " I now observed how the women began to paint themselves, formerly a most ignominious thing."

As for patching, it was universal, and evidently only another " snare " for the feminine Quaker mind ! We learn from Pepys (May 1, 1667) of the patching of one maid:

That which I did see and wonder at with reason, was to find Pegg Pen in a new coach, with only her husband's pretty sister

---

* Beck and Ball, " London Friends' Meetings," p. 77.
† "Anatomie of Abuses," p. 200.
‡ Ashton. " Social Life in Reign of Queen Anne," p. 118.

[Margaret Lowther] with her, both patched and very fine, and in much the finest coach in the park. . . . When we had spent half an hour in the park, we went out again, . . . and so home, where we find the two young ladies come home and their patches off. I suppose Sir W. Pen do not allow of them in his sight!

The "stay-maker" was the companion of the wig-maker; there are several Quakers whose names appear in the old London records as "stay-makers," or "bodice-makers." They advertised "both wooden and whalebone corset-busks." When the wig-makers ceased to be found among the Quakers, the bodice-makers pursued their way alone, that trade not being under condemnation, which only served to ruin the health, and was less conspicuous than the wig. "Fashion babies" have been alluded to; these merit more than a passing notice. They were models of costume, originally sent by Paris modistes to London and other cities of large population, displaying the very latest ideas in dress. The fashion plate was then far in the future, and even the Quakers employed this method of communicating their ideas as to the "proper thing" in drab to their country friends, or, as in the case of the doll model that was given to Stephen Grellet, to other communities of their own sect.

Several of these dolls have been kindly loaned me for examination. Just as Mademoiselle Martin, a famous modiste of the time of Marie Antoinette, was in the habit of sending doll models of the latest style, called "babies," to the most distant parts of Europe, so these quaint little Quaker dolls served to show the distant friend what was worn at the metropolis. There were, as we have seen, many changes of style in Quaker dress. The difference between them and the "world's people " lay in the magnitude and profundity of the question, relatively speaking; for quite as much thought and expenditure of time and money went into the alteration of a pleat in the Quaker bonnet, or a flap on the Quaker coat, as ever entered into the construction of a Paris " confection." Of these models— for it is a mistake to call them dolls, since they were anything but toys—one, for instance, is in the exact dress of Rebecca Jones, a well-known Philadelphia Friend, who lived from 1739 to 1818. She wears the bonnet with soft crown and a very large cape spreading in three points down the back and to the tip of each shoulder. The crown of another bonnet made about 1790, still extant, has a double box-pleat at top in center and four pleats down the side, clearly showing the coming stiff pleats in the " coal-scuttle " of later development. " Patty Rutter " is also a doll with a serious purpose, dressed in 1782 by Miss Sarah Rutter, of Philadelphia, and sent to Mrs. Samuel Adams, of Quincy, Massachusetts. It was presented to the Museum in Independence Hall in 1845. The doll is in Quaker dress, consisting of white silk bonnet and shawl, and drab silk gown. At her side hangs a chatelaine, with watch and pencil. The doll and her costume are still intact. The most interesting of all these models, however, is that of the Grellet family. Stephen Grellet was a famous French Quaker, who, as Étienne de Grellet du Mabillier, escaped from Limoges, his patrician father's home, at the time of the French revolution, and with a brother took refuge in América. Meeting with the Quakers, he became convinced of their principles, and at the time of his death was one of their most famous preachers. He was in England in the year 1816, intending to visit the French at Congénies in France, where was a little community remarkably in sympathy with the Friends, although having had no communication with them originally. English Friends desired to aid his efforts to build up their small meeting. The Quaker women of London, therefore, made and dressed for them a model in wax of a properly gowned woman Friend. Some untoward event recalled the preacher to his American home before he succeeded in the accomplishment of his original purpose. Upon his arrival, the doll was discovered, to his astonishment, in one of his trunks. When he wrote to ask how to dispose of the doll, the reply was: " Give her to thy little daughter." That " little daughter," living in New Jersey until July, 1901, to the great age of ninety years, was herself the authority for this story of " Rachel," as the beautiful doll has always been called. The fine rolled hem of the cap-border bears witness to the exquisite needle-work of the last century.

An increasing manifestation of the love of dress was marked throughout the colonies. The Friends from England noted this with an anxious eye, and in nearly all the meetings in America may be found records dealing with that tendency. Finally, Friends of Philadelphia Yearly Meeting, then held at Burlington, New Jersey, issued the following note of warning:

From Women ffriends at the Yearly Meeting held at Burlington, The 21st. of the 7th. Month, 1726.

To Women ffriends at the Several Quarterly & Monthly Meetings belonging to the same,—Greeting.

Dear and Well-beloved Sisters:

A Weighty Concern coming upon many ffaithful ffriends at this Meeting, In Relation to divers undue Liberties that are too frequently taken by some yt. walck among us, & are Accounted of us, We are Willing in the pure Love of Truth wch. hath Mercifully Visited our Souls, Tenderly to Caution & Advise ffriends against those things which we think Inconsistent with our Ancient Christian Testimony of Plainness in Apparel &c., Some of which we think it proper to Particularize.

As first, That Immodest ffashion of hooped Pettycoats, or ye. imitation of them, Either by Something put into their Pettycoats to make ym sett full, or Wearing more than is Necessary, or any other Imitation Whatsoever, Which we take to be but a Branch Springing from ye. same Corrupt root of Pride.

And also That None of Sd ffriends Accustom themselves to wear their Gowns with Superfluous ffolds behind, but plain and Decent. Nor to go without Aprons, Nor to wear Superfluous Gathers or Pleats in their Capps or Pinners, Nor to wear their heads drest high behind, Neither to Cut or Lay their hair on ye fforehead or Temples.

And that ffriends are careful to avoid Wearing of Stript Shoos, or Red or White heel'd Shoos, or Clogs, or Shoos trimmed wh. Gawdy Colours.

Likewise, That all ffriends be Careful to Avoid Superfluity of Furniture in their Houses, And as much as may be to refrain Using Gawdy floured or Stript Callicos and Stuffs.

And also that no ffriends Use ye Irreverent practice of taking Snuff, or handing Snuff boxes one to Another in Meetings.

Also That ffriends Avoid ye Unnecessary use of ffans* in Meetings, least it Divert ye mind from ye more Inward & Spiritual Exercise wch. all ought to be Concern'd in.

And also That ffriends do not Accustom themselves to go in bare Breasts or bare Necks.

There is Likewise a Tender Concern upon or minds to recommend unto all ffriends, the Constant use of ye plain Language It being a Branch of our Ancient Christian Testimony, for wch. many of or Worthy Elders underwent deep Sufferings in their Day As they Likewise Did because they could not give ye Com-

---

* "Ffans" first came to New England in 1714, so were not new in Pennsylvania and New Jersey at this time, although they were not in common use before 1750, and the Friends considered them very gay.

mon Salutation by Bowing and Cringing of ye Body wch. we
Earnestly desire ffriends may be Careful to Avoid.

And we farther Tenderly Advise and Exhort That all ffriends
be careful to Maintain Love and Unity and to Watch against
Whispering and Evil Surmisings One against Another, and to keep
in Humility, That Nothing be done through Strife or Vainglory,
and yt. those who are Concerned to take an oversight over the
fflock, Do it not as Lords over God's heritage, but as Servants
to ye Churches.

Dear Sisters, These Things we Solidly recommend to yor Care
and Notice In a Degree of yt. Divine Love wch hath previously
Manifested Itself for ye Redemption of a [MS. illegible] ye Vain
Conversations, Customs, & Fashions yt. are in ye World, That
we might be unto ye Lord, A Chosen Generation, A Royal Priest-
hood, An Holy Nation, A Peculair People, Shewing forth ye
Praises of him who hath called us out of Darkness into his Mar-
vellous Light, that We may all walck as Children of the Light
& of ye Day, Is ye Earnest Desire of our Souls.

We Conclude wth. ye Salutation of Unfeigned Love, yor ffriends
and Sisters.

Signed on behalf & by ordr. of ye sd. Meeting By

HANNAH HILL.

The " surprise " fan was made with an unexpected
joint, like the early parasols.   Ann Warder notes the
constant and needless use of fans, and with some com-
placency, remarks upon her own forbearance in the matter, " lest it should prove a disturbance to others."
Only two days after her arrival from England, under
date 9th of June, 1786, she wrote, " Such a general use
of fans my eyes never beheld.   You scarcely see a
woman without one.   And in winter, I am told, they
visit with them as a plaything."   She noticed a
child with a dirty face playing in the street.   The
mother " did not wash its face in the daytime for fear
of spoiling its complexion ! "   " Their mode of dressing children in Philadelphia," she regards, as " not so
becoming as with us.   I have scarcely seen a White

" *Going to Meeting in 1750.*"

From an original photograph.

A Quaker Wedding, 1820.

After the original painting by Percy Bigland in possession of
Isaac H. Clothier, Wynnewood, Pennsylvania.

Frock since my arrival. Not a woman has visited me but was elegant enough for any Bride, indeed we could almost persuade ourselves that was the case from so much saluting."

No costume was more important for the Quaker woman of the seventeenth and eighteenth centuries than that designed for use on horseback. This was even more the case in the colonies than in England, where, in London, at least, the sedan chair and the coach were cosmopolitan luxuries enjoyed very early. Country Friends, however, had to ride everywhere, and a woman, and especially a woman minister, if she traveled at all, must of necessity be a good horsewoman. The riding hood, with cape or long cloak attached— called a " Nithesdale " or " Capuchin," respectively— was worn over the ordinary dress, the skirt of which was often protected by a " safeguard." Mrs. Earle defines a " safeguard " as an " outside petticoat of heavy linen or woollen stuff, worn over other skirts to protect them from mud in riding on horseback." Ann Warder wrote of the Quaker women of Pennsylvania, in 1786, " They are very shiftable. They ride by themselves with a safeguard, which, when done with, is tied to the saddle, and the horse hooked to a rail, standing all meeting time as still as their riders sit." The " safeguard " seems to have disappeared in New England after 1750, indicating the introduction of the riding habit, which was appearing in England, and exciting the ridicule of the cynical Dean of St. Patrick's,*

---

* "I did not like [Miss Forester], although she be a toast and was dressed like a man." Swift, Journal to Stella, August 11th, 1711. The riding habit, which was the dress Swift alluded to, had just come in. Pepys, 1666, had also described the ladies in the galleries at Whitehall, in doublets, with periwigs and hats.

and others. The flat beaver hat, with very broad brim, and crown not two inches in height, was much worn for riding, and its contemporary cloak is of heavy grey stuff, the originals from which the illustration was taken being known to be over one hundred and fifty years old.

An accompaniment of the riding costume was the riding-mask, vizor, or, as usually written, "vizzard."

Lady's Riding Hat.

It was of this that Fox wrote, "Away with your unnecessary buttons," "your skimming-dish hats," "*vizzards,*" etc. He is probably referring also to the "vizzard" which was used as well in walking, and at one time worn hanging by a ribbon or cord at the side. In 1645, we are told, the Puritans of Plymouth, Mass., for "some unaccountable reason," forbade them to their people. We should think that the reason of extravagance might have proved as sufficient with them as with the Quakers. For old Stubbes, not long before this, had been making his ultra-Puritanical strictures on almost all varieties of English dress, and he thus scores the visors:

When they vse to ride abroad, they haue visors made of veluet (or in my iudgment they may rather be called inuisories) where-with they couer all their faces, hauing holes made in them agaynst their eies, whereout they looke. So that if a man that knew not their guise before, shoulde chaunce to meete one of theme, he would thinke he mette a monster or a deuill; for face he can see none, but two broad holes against their eyes with glasses in them. Thus they prophane the name of God, and liue in all kinde of voluptuousnesse and pleasure, worse than euer did the heathen.*

The mystery of their attachment while riding, with possibly both hands occupied with a restless horse, is solved by learning that the article had a silver mouth-piece, by which the teeth of the wearer held it in place, leaving her free to grasp the reins or the pillion, as the case might be. There was no protection from rain or sleet in those days before the umbrella, and a rainy-day costume was imperative. All sorts of devices were permissible.

> Good housewives all the winter's rage despise,
> Defended by the riding-hood's disguise.
>
> .   .   .   .   .   .
>
> Why should I teach the maid, when torrents pour
> Her head to shelter from the sudden shower?
> Nature will best her ready hand inform
> With her spread petticoat to fence the storm.
>
> Gay. " Trivia."

Reference has elsewhere been made to the gay color-ing of the clothing among the early Puritans in New England, but by the middle of the eighteenth century their garb was generally as " sad " in color as their or-dinary life was in tone. A pleasant contrast to them

---

*Philip Stubbes, " Anatomie of Abuses," p. 76. Ed. 1586.

are the homely Dutch Vrouws of New Amsterdam,
who wore gowns of the gayest tints, as they went
clinking along the streets in their heavy footgear. The
Quaker women of the colonies seem to have more in
common with the latter than with the Puritans, despite
their sobriety of living. Scarlet cloaks found their
way to America very early in the history of Penn's
colony, and there seems to have been much latitude in
dress. The wealthy women Friends in Pennsylvania
in the days of the Founder, dressed far more expen-
sively and elaborately than they ever did at a later
date; they flourished about in " white satin petticoats,
worked in flowers, pearl satin gowns, or peach-colored
satin cloaks; their white necks were covered with delicate lawn, and they wore gold chains and seals, en-
graven with their arms." Miss Repplier tells us that
Sarah Logan Norris, the wife of Isaac Norris, of Fair-
hill, wore a gown of deep blue. Mary, the daughter
of Thomas Lloyd, who married Isaac Norris, the elder,
wore blue and crimson; while her granddaughter,
Mary Dickinson, wore deep red. All these women
were Quakers of the best families in the country. It
is worth while to note that the daughter of Mary Dickinson, Maria Logan, was far more plain than her
mother or grandmother had been, showing a growing
tendency of the Quakers to emphasize plainness, and an
increasing attention to uniformity of garb among their
members. The presence of the Founder seems to have
had much the effect of the residence of the sovereign
in a small estate. His courtly dress and manners had
their inevitable effect upon the Quakers, whether in
London or Philadelphia; and had it been possible to

prolong his life through the next century, his people might have been spared much of their narrow policy, political as well as social, by the aid of his sane and experienced advice. There is universal testimony to the beauty and picturesqueness of the young Quakeresses of the aristocracy in the early days. The portrait of " The Fair Quaker," Hannah Middleton Gurney, whose costume was identical with that of Gulielma Springett, William Penn's first wife,* is that of a surpassingly handsome woman; and the Frenchman, Brissot, wrote of the Philadelphia Quakeresses many years after at the time of the Revolution, when dress was plainer among them:

These youthful creatures whom nature has so well endowed, whose charm has so little need of art, wear the finest muslins and silks. Oriental luxury would not disdain the exquisite textures in which they take delight.

The Frenchman did not fail to admire anything so artistic, and the Duc de la Rochefoucauld is the next to express himself, adding, " Ribbons please the young Quakeresses, and are the greatest enemies of the sect." †

Many agreed with the writer who not long before had said:

Behold the smart Quaker that looks in the glass,
Her hair doth all other companions surpass;
You deform your sweet faces, I vow and declare;
You should cut off your lappets and burn your false hair.‡

---

*See explanatory note regarding this portrait in Maria Webb's " Penns and Penningtons of the Seventeenth Century," to which the engraving of " Guli " Penn forms the frontispiece. It is quite distinct from the engraving with the same title, here reproduced.

† Agnes Repplier, " Philadelphia ; The Place and the People," p. 286.

‡ " The Mountain of Hair," 1760. Percy Soc. Vol. XXVII., p. 245.

Our great-grandmothers, if we may judge by the clothes that have come down to us, were, as a rule, smaller women than the average in these days of their tall and athletic descendants.

The private Diary of Ann, wife of James Whitall, of Red Bank, New Jersey, under date, 21st 12 mo., 1760, has the following:

Oh, will there ever be a Nehemiah raised at our meeting to mourn and grieve! Oh, the fashions and running into them! The young men wearing their hats set up behind, and next it's likely will be a ribbon to tie their hair up behind; the girls in Pennsylvania have their necks set off with a black ribbon; a sorrowful sight indeed! . . . There is this day Josiah Albertson's son, all the son he has, and his hat is close up behind!

A little later, 3 mo. 18, 1762:

Oh, I think, could my eyes run down with tears always for the abomination of the times. So much excess of tobacco; and tea is as bad, so much of it, and they will pretend they can't do without it; and there is the calico—Oh, the calico! . . . I think tobacco and tea and calico may all be set down with the negroes, one as bad as the other.*

The mournful strain in which the above is written was somewhat characteristic of the more sober plain folk among the Quakers of the last century. Many old letters exist in which are recorded prolonged wails and groanings in spirit over bonnet strings, hat-bands, shoe-buckles, and such momentous matters, all treated with the utmost gravity. Great interests were at stake in both England and America at these periods; but the Friends withdrew themselves from contact with outside interests of all sorts; and this, in addition to the greater isolation of each little community than in modern times, due to the difficulty of travel, tended

---

* Hannah Whitall Smith, " The Life of John M. Whitall."

to cultivate a feeling of their own importance in the world, and to the exaggeration of details in their little neighborhoods; so that the appearance of a man on the street with a new cock to his hat, or of a young woman with a black ribbon at her neck, shook the community to its foundations! It is amusing to read, in the editor's comments on the above diary, that at the very time the writer was so bewailing the worldliness of a black ribbon, she herself sat under the gallery of Woodbury meeting, arrayed in a straw bonnet lined with pink silk! After all, there is no standard of perfect plainness. The matter is entirely a relative one.

In the month of May, 1771, Isaac Collins, of Burlington, N. J., married Rachel Budd, of Philadelphia, at the "Bank Meeting," in that city. His wedding dress was a coat of peach blossom cloth, the great skirts of which had outside pockets; it was lined throughout with quilted white silk. The large waistcoat was of the same material. He wore small clothes, knee buckles, silk stockings and pumps—a cocked hat surmounted the whole. The bride, who is described as "lovely in mind and person," wore a light blue brocade, shoes of the same material, with very high heels —not larger at the sole than a gold dollar—and sharply pointed at the toes. Her dress was in the fashion of the day, consisting of a robe, long in the back, with a large hoop. A short blue bodice with a white satin stomacher embroidered in colors, had a blue cord laced from side to side. On her head she wore a black mode hood lined with white silk, the large cape extending over the shoulders. Upon her return from meeting after the ceremony, she put on a thin white apron of ample dimensions, tied in front with a large blue bow. The gaiety of this display positively takes our breath, particularly when we reflect that the bride had once belonged in John Woolman's own meeting. And yet, it only serves to show that the entire question of dress is relative, custom and precedent usually dictating what is unlawful, the whole matter being arbitrary to a startling degree. Our heart goes out to this beautifully picturesque Quaker couple, of whom the groom was already making a name for himself in the printer's art, and who shortly after issued the colonial currency of New Jersey in connection with the greater Franklin.* Apparently, the plain Friends were so accustomed to brilliant dressing in the neighborhood of Philadelphia, a very gay town in that day, that they did not take alarm at the colors introduced on this occasion, despite all they had said and written on the subject of dress in their official character.

That the younger Quakers followed the changes of Dame Fashion has been, we think, fully demonstrated. The wedding of Isaac Collins and Rachel Budd carried out the styles then prevailing. The ideal painting by Percy Bigland, "A Quaker Wedding," historically correct in its representation, shows a dress plainly influenced by the times, as the "empire" gown of the bride indicates. The "Two Friends," belongs to the years between 1835 and 1840, and since that time the present generation can refer to the costumes of their own parents. Older people have worn the modern plain bonnet and shawl for fifty or sixty

---

*I am indebted to the great-granddaughter of this picturesque couple for the description, which is authentic.

years. Before that time, the same bonnet had a soft crown; and a long hooded cloak—cloth in winter and silk in summer—was substituted for the shawl. The Quakers have always shown their exquisite taste in choice of materials, and have instinctively realized that nothing but the best stuffs would lend themselves with dignity to the severe simplicity of their garb. This could have been better realized some thirty years ago, when each of our great cities supported at least one large shop where Quaker goods exclusively were sold. The fact that the Quakers can now be served at any shop speaks volumes for either their deterioration or their progress—depending upon one's point of view.

By the time of the Revolution, Philadelphia far surpassed all other towns in the colonies with its extravagance and luxury of living, winding up with the " Meschianza "—that pageant whose tradition is still rehearsed in the ears of modern townsfolk, sounding more like a page from the fairy tales of the Middle Ages than actual happenings in the city of Penn. A Hessian officer, writing of the ladies of America at that time, says,*

They are great admirers of cleanliness,and keep themselves well shod. They friz their hair every day and gather it up on the back of the head into a chignon, at the same time puffing it up in front. They generally walk about with their heads uncovered, and sometimes but not often wear some light fabric on their hair. Now and then some country nymph has her hair flowing down behind her, braided with a piece of ribbon. Should they go out, even though they be living in a hut, they throw a silk wrap about themselves and put on gloves. They also put on some well made and stylish little sunbonnet, from which their roguish eyes have a most fascinating way of meeting yours. In

---

* Alice Morse Earle, " Costume of Colonial Times," p. 31.

the English colonies the beauties have fallen in love with red silk or woolen wraps.

A letter of Miss Rebecca Franks, a Philadelphia belle visiting in New York in 1778, speaks thus of society there in that year:

1776.
(After Martin.)

You can have no idea of the life of continued amusement I live in. I can scarce have a moment to myself. I have stole this while everybody is retired to dress for dinner. I am but just come from under Mr. J. Black's hands, and most elegantly dressed am I for a ball this evening at Smith's, where we have one every Thursday. . . . The dress is more rediculous and pretty than anything I ever saw—a great quantity of different coloured feathers on the head at a time beside a thousand other things. The hair dressed very high, in the shape Miss Vining's was the night we returned from Smith's--the Hat we found in your Mother's closet wou'd be of a proper size. I have an afternoon cap with one wing, tho' I assure you I go less in the fashion than most of the ladies—no being dressed without a hoop.

The Journal of Elizabeth Drinker, of Philadelphia, under date " December 15, 1777," says:

Peggy York called this morning. . . . She had on the highest and most rediculous headdress that I have yet seen.

A little later, July 4, 1778:

A very high headdress was exhibited thro' ye streets this afternoon, on a very dirty woman, with a mob after her with drums etc. by way of ridiculing that very foolish fashion.

The Two Friends.

After the Engraving by Bouvier, London. About 1835.

The Fair Quaker.

London, *1782.*

In 1786 Ann Warder's Journal describes similar extravagance:

"Came to call"—a fine girl called the perfection of America but her being drest fantastical to the greatest degree and painted like a doll destroyed every pretension to Beauty, in my mind.

Such extravagance recalls the old poem:

THE LADIES' HEAD-DRESS.

Give Chloe a bushel of horse-hair and wool,
Of paste and pomatum a pound,
Ten yards of gay ribbon to deck her sweet skull,
And gauze to encompass it round.

Of all the bright colours the rainbow displays
Be those ribbons which hang on her head,
Be her flounces adapted to make the folks gaze,
And about the whole work be they spread.

Let her flaps fly behind, for a yard at the least;
Let her curls meet just under her chin;
Let these curls be supported, to keep up the jest,
With an hundred, instead of one, pin.

Let her gown be tuck'd up to the hip on each side;
Shoes too high for to walk, or to jump;
And, to deck the sweet creature complete for a bride,
Let the cork-cutter make her a rump.

Thus finish'd in taste, while on Chloe you gaze,
You may take the dear charmer for life;
But never undress her—for, out of her stays
You'll find you have lost half your wife.*

An American in London at the end of the last century, whether Quaker or not, was bound to have some surprises in contrasting the styles at home and abroad.

---

* From Publications of Percy Society, Vol. XXVII., p. 259. Printed first in " London Magazine " for 1777, and very popular.

In 1781, Lady Cathcart, an American by birth, wrote of London fashions:

They wear for morning a white poloneze or a dress they call a Levete [Levite] which is a kind of gown and Peticote with long sleeves made with scarcely any pique in the back, and worn with a sash tyed on the left side. They make these in winter of white dimity, and in summer of muslin with chintz borders.

We are told that the " robe-levite " imitated this garment, and that the " monkey-tailed levite " had a curiously twisted train, and was a French fashion.* Our " Fair Quaker " of this date wears what is no doubt a " Levite." Did its name help to make it seem less worldly?

George and Sarah (Hill) Dillwyn, very plain Friends from Philadelphia, went over to visit their English relatives in London soon after the peace was signed. Her letters to her family at home in New Jersey are the observations of an alert, lively woman, to whose philosophical mind the gay capital served as an amusement, but not in the least a temptation. Her opportunities for observation were of the best. She writes to her sister, M. Morris, dating her letter. " London, 4 12th. 1785 ":

I find it in vain to keep pace here with the nice dames, so don't care a fig about it; let us be dressed as we will, I find the best of them take a great deal more notice of us than either of us desires.†

They mention their reticules—spelt preferably by all, apparently, " ridicule; " these side pockets must match the gown, with tassel and strings.

" When writing of women," said Diderot, " we should dip our pen in the rainbow, and throw over each

---

* Mrs. Earle, " Costume of Colonial Times," p. 152.
† " Letters of the Hill Family," edited by J. J. Smith, p. 256.

line the powder of the butterfly's wing, instead of
sand ! " No such ethereal notion is left of woman in
these athletic days of the golfing girl, but it is not so
long since exercise was a disgrace, and to seem to live
on anything more substantial than air, a crime against
good taste. Gowns, of course, partook of the general
æsthetic tendency, and the period of classicism in dress
left its imprint on the garb even of the Quaker ladies
of the early part of this century. Fashions as a rule
change gradually, but at the French Revolution they
made a sudden revolt, and down came the " high
heads " and the " poufs au sentiment," the latter a
pleasing structure some four feet high, representing
at the wearer's whim, gardens and trees, and ships under full sail in billowy seas of gauze, or models of their
nursery and babies and all their pet animals. The reaction went to the other extreme, when Paris sought
to reproduce Greek simplicity; the " statuesque "
effects that resulted might have caused even a Greek
statue to blush. The desired effect was attained by discarding to the limit of decency, and even beyond it,
all possible undergarments. None too many, according to our hygienic ideas in this day, had ever been
worn. But a scanty cambric petticoat in the last days
of the last century was quite the heaviest undergar-
ment possible. The clinging draperies that resulted
displayed a curious commingling of classical names;
and one fine lady is quoted as wearing at the same time
in 1809, " a robe à la Didon, a Carthage Cymar, and a
Spartan Diadem." Tito, Daphne, Ariadne, Calypso,
Diana and the whole Greek array were levied upon to
distinguish different styles; and even Medusa lent her

name to a coiffure! The only thing to be said in favor
of this riot of classicism was that it put an abrupt end
to cocked hats, wigs, pigtails and hair powder. Hoops
became past horrors, as did expanded petticoats; but
while the less enthusiastic English refused to be quite
so unrestrained in dress as their neighbors across the
channel, they followed sufficiently far to attain a high
disdain for any underclothing that interfered with
statuesque effects, and perilous indeed must have been
the results in the unfriendly English climate. Gauze
and silks and tiffanys and taffetas, India muslins and
delicate gossamers were considered heavy enough for
winter wear by our English grandmothers, who, poor
things, killed themselves off before their time and trans-
mitted many an ill to their descendants as a tribute to
Dame Fashion. Shoes came from France, and were of
finest kid, for by some unaccountable mental bias it
was no more possible then than it is now for the English to make a graceful shoe. Rouge was described as
an "animating appendage" to the toilette, and cold
water was regarded as an enemy to good looks—" the
natural enemy to a smooth skin!" Prince Jerome
Bonaparte married Miss Elizabeth Patterson on Christ-
mas eve, 1803. A gentleman who was present wrote:

All the clothes worn by the bride might have been put in my
pocket. Her dress was of muslin richly embroidered, of extremely fine texture. Beneath her dress she wore but a single garment.*

The classical craze wore itself out, as crazes will.
The only reason that it has here been referred to is because the scanty supply of underclothing which it per-

* Mrs. Hunt, "Our Grandmothers' Gowns," p. 15.

mitted caused our Quaker grandmothers many an ill,
in the tradition left them that true refinement demanded an attire too airy to be compatible with the
sharp changes of an English or American winter. Nobody wore woollen garments in the early nineteenth
century, and for a long time cloth was regarded as very
unfeminine even for an outside wrap. Linen was universal, and silk stockings with the thinnest lasting, or
" prunella " shoes and slippers, with soles of paper-like
thickness, were the usual foot-covering in houses full
of draughts caused by open fires. Carpet or " list "
shoes were donned by old ladies for snow and ice, and
clogs and pattens were worn by the belles of the day.
To be sure, heavy fur pelisses were worn in bitter
weather, but were at once thrown aside on entering the
house.

We find that calicoes with gay and fanciful designs
became very fashionable after the Revolution in America; and it is no doubt to this mode that the Diary of
Ann Whitall refers. An old newspaper says, " Since
the peace, calico has become the general fashion of our
country women, and is worn by females of all condi-
tions at all seasons of the year, both in town and country." The French calicoes were delicate in texture and
color, and were said to have been so popular that they
were even worn in the freezing cold churches and meeting houses in the dead of a New England winter. There
was nothing modest about some of the designs, if we
may believe the old advertisements, which describe pat-
terns called " liberty peak," "Covent Garden crossbar,"
" Ranelagh half-moon," and a " fine check inclosing
Four Lions Rampant and three flours de Luce." Some

were adorned with the portraits of political heroes, like Washington and Franklin. We are further told that these designs were stamped by blocks for the hand, which are still in existence.* The New England mantua-maker of 1668 charged eight shillings per day —a fair comparison with a modern seamstress—and the dressmaker who made up the calicoes a hundred years later got no more. A young married woman, who was a Friend, wrote to her sister from Washington, Dutchess County, New York, Seventh month 13th, 1828:

> Yesterday was Preparative Meeting. The clerk was a young girl, I think not twenty years of age, dressed in a painted muslin, with a very large figure, almost white, a cape with a small transparent handkerchief round the neck, and a bonnet of white silk in the real English fashion, gathered very full, and altogether the most showy looking clerk I ever saw. . . .
>
> I went over to the store yesterday and bought a real calico gown, a dress one,—light, to put on afternoons, when it is too cold for gingham, as it mostly is in this elevated region. I find it necessary to be pretty much dressed all the time if one is to keep up with the custom of the house. Even Mother made up a white apron, as she says she did not bring one, thinking they w'd not be worn here, but she finds her mistake.

The large figures became more modest later on. On the back of an old letter, dated 1833, in my grandmother's handwriting, I find the following memorandum: " Very small figures are the fashion here now for waistcoats and for gowns too."
Just before this she had written:

> I can't bear to wear anything but crepe handkerchiefs this hot weather. . . . Short sleeves only are wearable either. I have not yet ventur'd to cut off more than one pair, but think I shall.

---

* Alice Morse Earle, " Costume of Colonial Times," p. 74.

These calicoes and figured stuffs were so famous for their large design that what to-day would seem to us a very conspicuous figure, was considered proper for Rebecca Jones to wear in Philadelphia on the occasion of her first appearance in the ministry. The original material is really a printed brown linen; the name of calico seems to have been of general application to stuffs of this sort. The early Friends had borne their testimony against these flights of fancy,* but " flour'd and figur'd things " have seemed to recur in feminine costume in some form ever since the days of Mother Eve.

It is hard to imagine the Quaker woman without her shawl; yet that article of dress was not worn in this country until 1784, when " a rich assortment of shawls " was advertised in Salem, Mass. The garment was the result of the East India trade, just beginning at this time, and was not worn in Europe much before the opening of the present century. An observant attender of Quaker meetings must have noted the manner in which the plain Quakeress sometimes takes her seat, as, with a hand behind her, palm outward, she gives an indescribable little " *flip* " to the corner of her shawl, to turn it up behind at the moment of seating herself to avoid wrinkles in the tail! The air with which that " *flip* " is sometimes given by a quick-motioned young woman, is levity itself. And none but the initiated can know of the art involved in donning the plain shawl

---

* " 1st of 5 mo., 1693, Minute 7th. Before a minute offered to the Quarterly Meeting, concerning Fr'ds making, ordering, or selling striped cloths silks, or stuffs, or any sort of flour'd, figur'd things of different colours. It is the judgment of the Quarterly Meet'g that Friends ought to stand clear of such things." Unlocated. Copy by H. Hull, New York, 1850.

properly; the depth of the three folds exactly in the center of the back of the neck, and the size of the pin that holds them; the pin on the tip of each shoulder, to hold the fullness in sufficient firmness, without pulling, and without showing that it *is* a pin; and the momentous decision whether the point of the shawl is exactly in the middle, or not—indeed, there are impressive moments in the lives of all women.

Some form of cloak, usually hooded, was universal before the simplicity of the shawl commended itself at first sight to the Quakeress of the nineteenth century. The return of the Emperor Napoleon from his campaign in Egypt, bringing to Josephine some beautiful cashmere shawls, gave that garment a great vogue in 1807. The Empress took an immense fancy to the shawl, and there was a time at which she was scarcely ever seen without one in the morning. It is said that "she had about five hundred, for many of which she had given as much as ten or twelve thousand francs. The Emperor did not like to see her wrapped in her shawls within doors, and sometimes pulled them off and threw them in the fire, but she always sent for another."

The " Belle Assemblée " discourages the shawl. It says:

It is only wonderful, that such an article of dress should ever have found its path to fashionable adoption in the various circles of British taste. In its form, nothing can be more opposed to every principle of refined taste, or carry less the appearance of that elegant simplicity at which it aims. It is calculated much more to conceal and vulgarize than to display or regulate the contour of an elegant form, and is totally destitute of every idea of ease, elegance, or dignity. Whatever charms it may have for the sickly taste of the tawny BELLES of the torrid zone, nothing but that witching beauty which occasionally veils itself in the rusticity and homeliness (like the sun, its mists and clouds) that it may dazzle anew, with the refulgent splendor of its taste and charm, could render even tolerable the introduction of an habiliment which turns any female NOT beautiful and elegant into an absolute DOWDY. IT is the very contrast to the flowing elegance of the Grecian costume, whose light and transparent draperies so admirably display the female form.*

A Quaker poet thus expressed himself later:

> Observe yon belles! behold the waspish waist!
> See the broad bishop spreading far behind;
> The shawl immense, with uncouth figures graced,
> And veil loose waving in the playful wind;
> Mark the huge bonnets, stuck on hills of hair,
> Like meteors streaming in the turbid air.†

The impressions of the life and manners of the seven sisters Gurney, of Norwich, England, by A. J. C. Hare,‡ show the Quaker influence at work on a set of young people to whom no privileges of culture or refinement had ever been denied. The family to which belonged Joseph John and his talented sister, Elizabeth Gurney, better known by her married name of Elizabeth Fry, may well merit a little attentive study. Harriet Martineau describes the sisters as "a set of dashing young people, dressing in gay riding habits and scarlet boots, and riding about the country to balls and gaieties of all sorts. Accomplished and charming young ladies they were, and we children used to hear whispered gossip about the effect of their charms on heart-stricken young men." The seven are said to

---

*1807, quoted by Mrs. A. W. Hunt, in " Our Grandmothers' Gowns," p. 28.

† Samuel J. Smith, of Hickory Grove, N. J.

‡ Augustus J. C. Hare, " The Gurneys of Earlham."

have linked arms, and in their scarlet * riding-habits, in which they scoured the country side on their ponies, stopped the great mail-coach from ascending the neighboring hill! The brother Daniel states in his " Reminiscences," that his four younger sisters never wore bonnets on the Earlham grounds, but put on little red cloaks in which they ran about as they liked. Louisa Gurney (afterward Mrs. Samuel Hoare) writes, June 5th, 1797, " In the evening I dressed up in Quaker things, but I felt far too ashamed to say or act anything," so strong was the influence of the Quaker spirit. The same seven sat in a row in front of the ministers' gallery at Norwich Meeting. One day Betsey (Elizabeth Fry) had on a pair of " new purple boots lined with scarlet," which sounds amazingly gorgeous to us at this day. Betsey was counting upon the delights of the shoes to console her through the tedium she anticipated. But as it proved, this was to be a memorable day to her. It was the fourth of February, 1798, and Betsey was eighteen. William Savery, the great American preacher, was present, and his sermon was so forceful and appealed so to her, that she became convinced of the truth of Quaker principles and became a Quaker from that time forth.

That same meeting seems to have shocked Friend Savery, for he wrote that he found it very gay for a Friends' meeting. " There were," he says, " about two hundred under our name, very few middle aged. I thought it the gayest meeting of Friends I ever sat in, and was quite grieved at it. . . . Marks of wealth and grandeur are too evident in several families in this

---

* " Kutusoff " mantles of scarlet cloth were much worn later.

place." Maria Edgeworth describes Elizabeth Fry after years had passed, in her "drab-colored silk cloak and plain borderless silk cap." When Joseph Fry first determined to marry Elizabeth Gurney, if it were possible, he saw her in a brown silk gown, with a black lace veil bound around her head like a turban, the ends pendant on one side of her face, and contrasting with her beautiful light brown hair. Richenda, her sister, writes of the "troutbecks" they were all wearing at the seaside in 1803. These were hats of that year. Red cloaks are mentioned, and the fashions of the time show the brilliant colors of wraps and all outside garments of the day to have been very startling. All except the plainest Quakers made some concession to the mode. Priscilla Gurney writes to Hannah, her sister, afterward the wife of Sir T. Fowell Buxton, "Chenda and I wear our dark gowns every day, and our aprons in the evening." This was in February, 1803. In 1805, Louisa Gurney writes to her sister, Elizabeth Fry, "I often seem to see thee in thy pink acorn gown attending to all thy flock in the dining room," etc. This "pink acorn gown" was probably a pattern similar to the calicoes and printed stuffs so popular among the Friends at the time, to which reference has already been made. We are told that in May, 1807, at the marriage of the Buxtons, "The house was overrun with bridesmaids in muslin cloaks and chip hats." In 1813, Katherine Fry says, "Our Aunts Catherine and Rachel (Gurney) wore no caps, but a headdress of crêpe folded turbanwise. Both were brown in the morning; in the afternoons, Aunt Catherine's were dark red; Aunt Rachel's, white. Aunt Rachel also frequently wore

white muslin dresses. They had few or no ornaments.
Aunt Catherine always wore dark or black silk, but
often with a red shawl. Aunt Priscilla, as a Friend,
was dressed in a dark silk or poplin gown, exquisitely
neat, finished and refined." The Aunt Catherine who
was the head of the family, while never a Quaker, always regarded the preferences of those who were of that
faith in her circle, and studied an elegant simplicity of
dress that was the admiration of her friends, seeking to
avoid any marked or startling contrasts among the very
varied views of the sisters.

Their intimate friend was the author, Amelia Opie;
that talented convert to the faith went into it with her
customary ardor, and the change from worldly garb
was made at one leap, when once she became convinced
of the necessity for the sacrifice of her love of color,
which, as the wife of the artist, John Opie, had been
more than ordinarily cultivated.* But she seems to
have seen in the simple elegance of her Quaker friends,
sufficient outlet for all artistic aspirations in the realm
of costume; and certainly no more stately women
could have been found in the King's domain to set off
the possibilities of silk and satin, when worn with grace
and distinction. As though partly in explanation of
what seemed to their friends an extraordinary step,
Southey wrote of Mrs. Opie:

I like her in spite of her Quakerism—nay, perhaps the better
for it. It must always be remembered amongst what persons
she had lived, and that religion was never presented to her in
a serious form until she saw it in drab.

---

* Joseph John Gurney, in writing of her at this time, says, " Great
was her agony of mind in view of changing her dress, and of addressing
her numerous friends and acquaintances by their plain names, and with
the humbling simplicity of thee and thou."

So remarkable a figure was that of Elizabeth Fry
in the elegant simplicity of Quaker dress, whether in
the prison of Newgate, or before the crowned heads of
Europe, that her dress has become fixed in the public
mind as the type of woman's Quaker costume. Elizabeth Fry writes to her husband from The Hague, after
an audience with the King and Queen, in 1847, " I
wore a dark plain satin, and a new fawn colored silk
shawl." At this time, however, it was no new thing
for Elizabeth Fry to wait upon royalty. Her first visit
to court was made in 1818, when Queen Charlotte commanded her presence at the Mansion House, upon
which occasion A. J. C. Hare says, " Royalty offered
its meed of approval at the shrine of mercy and good
works." The Queen's stature was diminutive; she was
covered with diamonds, her countenance lighted up
with an expression of the kindest benevolence. Elizabeth Fry's simple Quaker dress added to the height of
her tall figure. She was slightly flushed, but kept her
wonted calm. Her daughter wrote afterward:

They entered, Lady Harcourt in full court dress, on the arm
of Alderman Wood in scarlet gown; and then the Bishop of
Gloucester (Ryder) in lawn sleeves, leading our darling mother
in her plain Friend's cap, one of the light scarf cloaks worn by
plain Friends, and a dark silk gown. I see her now, her light
flaxen hair, a little flush in her face from the bustle and noise
she had passed through, and her sweet, lovely, placid smile.*

Ann Warder, whose interesting Journal covers three
years, from 1786 to 1789, among the Friends of Philadelphia and vicinity, gives us vivid pictures of life in
the young republic, and the privilege of quoting from

*A. J. C. Hare, " The Gurneys of Earlham."

its unpublished pages has been gladly availed of. She
tells us that upon landing from the ship Edward, in
New York, in 1786, they were taken at once to the
home of a Friend of the family. " The woman Friend
of the house came up, and as a mark of her welcome,
untied my cap to help strip me." At this period, Ann
Warder was twenty-eight. On being told that her appearance was singular, she explained that " countries
differed; riding dresses with us were very much worn,
and mine in England would be esteemed a plain one.
This is a specimen of their singularity on this Island
[Long Island]; scarce any had Buckles, and not a
looped hat did I see." When word reached Philadelphia by messenger of the arrival of John Warder and
his English wife, ten minutes sufficed to see their
Brother Jeremiah and his wife on their way to New
York to meet them. Haste probably accounts for the
appearance of the new arrival from the South, who is
thus described by the English woman, and contrasted
with her husband, his brother. She allows us to see
the unconventional dress of the Quaker of that day:

His dress unstudied, a Cocked Hat, Clumsy Boots, Brown cloth
large Breeches, Black Velvet Waistcoat, light old Cazemar [cassi-
mere] coat, handkerchie instead of stock which is tied on without much pains. Conceive J. W. [her husband] with his suit—
Nankeen Inexpressibles and white silk stockings, much more re-
sembling an English gentleman.

She adds:

The women I have seen at present appear Indolent, which may
perhaps be a reason for Mother Warder's bearing such a high
character for notability.

To be a " notable " housewife was to reach woman's
summit of social ambition at that day among the Quakers.

Got B. Parker to go out shoping with me. On our way happened of Uncle Head, to whom I complained bitterly of the dirty streets, declaring if I could purchase a pair of pattens, the singularity I would not mind. Uncle soon found me up an apartment, out of which I took a pair and trotted along quite Comfortable, crossing some Streets with the greatest ease, which the idea of had troubled me. My little companion was so pleased, that she wished some also, and kept them on her feet to learn to walk in them most of the remainder of the day.

The patten and clog are often spoken of interchangeably, but the clog is of vastly greater antiquity. The patten dates from the reign of Queen Anne, and is raised on a supporting ring; an excellent example may be seen in the museum of Independence Hall. Gay's charming explanation of their origin in his " Trivia " will, of course, come in mind. The clog in the illustration is from a beautiful pair carefully preserved in New Jersey. The hollow for the heel, and the preposterous elevation on the instep, designed to fill the arch of the foot in the companion shoe or slipper, are explained, and the illustration from our originals almost duplicated, in Fairholt's " Costume in England," which may be properly regarded as the final authority on matters of historical costume.

An insane woman remarked on Ann Warder's appearance when she visited the asylum in Philadelphia, that she (A. W.) was the " most clumsy woman in the party, but she believed it was because she had on too many petticoats."

I could not help being struck with two women Minister's appearance, both having Drab Silk Gowns, and Black Pasteboard Bonnets on. To see an old man stand up with a Mulberry Coat, Nankeen Waistcoat and Breeches with white stockings would look very Singular in England. My cap is the admiration of plain and gay.

A shopping expedition is recorded to find white leather mitts. " In not less than twenty [shops] did we ask for them before we succeeded; there is no place regular for different trades, as with us." The apron, as we have seen, had its day of popularity, and it is perhaps interesting to notice that the sleeve, which early in the seventeenth century was often a separate article of dress, after the old custom from the time of the Wars of the Roses, was apt to be of another color than the gown, and green was still the fashionable shade at this period. A famous old song of the time, in everybody's mouth, was " My Lady Greensleeves." It is mentioned by Shakespeare in the " Merry Wives of Windsor," where Falstaff says: " Let the sky rain potatoes; let it thunder to the tune of ' Green-Sleeves.' " (Act V., Scene 5.) Part of the old song is as follows: *

> Alas, my love, you do me wrong
> To cast me off discourteously;
> And I have loved you so long,
> Delighting in your company.
>
> Greensleeves was all my joy,
> Greensleeves was my delight;
> Greensleeves was my heart of Gold,
> And Who but Lady Greensleeves?
>
> I have been ready at your hand
> To grant whatever you would crave;
> I have both waged life and land
> Your goodwill for to have.
>
> Thou couldst desire no earthly thing
> But still thou hadst it readily.
> Thy music still to play and sing;
> And yet thou wouldst not love me.

---

* From " A Handful of Pleasant Delites," by Clement Robinson, 1584.

My men were clothèd all in green,
  And they did ever wait on thee,
All this was gallant to be seen,
  And yet thou wouldst not love me.

They set thee up, they took thee down,
  They served thee with humility,
Thy foot might not once touch the ground,
  And yet thou wouldst not love me.

Thy gown was of the grassy green,
  Thy sleeves of satin hanging by,
Which made thee be our harvest queen,
  And yet thou wouldst not love me.

Greensleeves, now farewell, adieu!
  God I pray to prosper thee!
For I am still thy lover true;
  Come once again and love me.

Walter Rutherford is quoted by Miss Wharton as objecting violently to " a late abominable fashion from London, of ladies like Washerwomen with their sleeves above their elbows." This was in 1790. Elbow sleeves were worn by all the plain Friends at one time; and long " mitts," reaching to the shoulder, elaborate and exquisitely plaited linen and fine muslin under-sleeves, - with the little gold link buttons to fasten them at the ends, are now in my possession. Through the latter half of the eighteenth, and the beginning of the nineteenth century, all plain women Friends wore gowns with low neck and short sleeves. This, I think, may be taken as an universal rule. The neck was protected by a dainty muslin or lawn handkerchief, folded across the bosom and pinned at the waist on each side. Over this was worn a soft silk shawl, and the shades of delicate gray or drab were often productive of the most exquis-ite effects, with a fresh young face. The young girl put on her cap before she was fairly grown up; and the first little girl sent to Westtown School in Pennsylvania, in 1799, wore a cap of

large proportions. No baby came into the world, whether of Quakerdom or of fashion, in the last century, without at once having its hairless little pate clapped into a more or less uncompromising cap, many of those still in existence being very elaborately embroidered. But we might forgive them for refusing to the little head the proper circulation of air, if they had not sinned in a far worse way

Hannah Hunt,
Westtown's First Scholar.
1799.
(Aetat 11.)

when they at once enclosed the poor little ribs in the most cruel of *stays.* For a long time, I tried to persuade myself that it was only the ultra-fashionable (or the Chinese) that so treated their offspring. But, alas! the pair of stiff, diminutive stays in my own possession has never been in the hands of the " world's people "; they come straight to me from a long line of Quaker ancestry, and I am reluctantly forced to believe that it was my own great-grandmother who refused freedom to the small ribs of her children, and laced the uncompromising implement of torture on her new-born infant. There are even now certain conservative women across the border in Canada, who still put their babies in tight jackets of this kind immediately after their birth, under the impression, which I suppose animated our great-grandmothers, that the small body needed " support," forsooth, much more than freedom!

When the children got to be of a suitable age for such instruction, literature like the following was read to them, with what effect, either on manners or morals, we are not told:

COUNSEL TO FRIENDS' CHILDREN.

Written at Coggeshall, Essex,
1745, by Anthony Purver.*

Dear little Friends, not tainted yet with ill,
By Sense not biassed, nor misled by Will;

.   .   .   .   .   .

Dress not to please, nor imitate the Nice;
Be like good Friends, and follow their Advice.
The rich man, gaily cloth'd, is now in Hell,
And Dogges did eat attirèd Jezebel.

.   .   .   .   .   .

Speak truly still, with Thou and Thee to One
As unto God; and feed the Pride in None;
Give them no flatt'ring Titles, tho' they scoff,
Lest God, provok'd, should quickly cut you off.
Him only did not the three Children fear,
And with their Hats before the King appear?

It may be set down as a safe rule, in seeking for a Quaker style or custom at any given time, to take the worldly fashion or habit of the period preceding. When the mode changes, and a style is dropped, the Quaker will be found just ready to adopt it, having by that time become habituated to its use. Of all this process he is quite unconscious; the philosophy of such matters having never been presented to him. He might, indeed, shrink from the suggestion that there is any philosophy of clothes, at all; but Carlyle has so

---

* Anthony Purver was born at Uphurstborn, near Whitechurch, in 1702, and died at Andover, Hampshire, 1777, aged 75. He was buried in the Friends' grounds at the latter place.

taught us. A very modern instance of this familiariz-
ing process and ultimate acceptance of what, on its first
appearance, is set down as a vain fashion, is the recent
adoption in one of the largest boarding-schools in the
society, and the only plain one, of the ordinary straw
sailor-hat among the girls, just as its popularity is on
the wane.

It will be noted that during the period following the
time of William Penn up to that of the summit of Elizabeth Fry's fame—an interval of nearly one hundred
and fifty years—there was no established type of
Quaker dress. No woman of the society had ever
come before the public eye in such a way as to impress
it with her personality, or stamp her character upon
the public mind. Elsewhere, I have indicated that the
witchcraft persecutions had caused the preaching
woman who was the contemporary of William Penn,
who came from the same class of society as the witch
who was hung or burned with such wanton cruelty on
both sides the Atlantic, and who wore a garb exactly
similar, to be seized upon as the type of our nursery
" witch." The most conspicuous instance was taken;
otherwise, we should have had the Quaker woman in
her cap and pointed hat, her apron and her high-heeled
shoes, standing beside William Penn upon our boxes
of Quaker oats. But during the interval that followed
the preaching of the first Quaker women, in the fields
and on upturned tubs in the halls and kitchens of the
early Quakers, no striking Quaker woman arose, until,
at Newgate, appeared Elizabeth Fry's beautiful figure
in its exquisite setting. The great movement in England toward prison reform organized by her noble

effort, has made her the type of the Quaker woman for all time.

A MEDITATION ON THE PRIDE OF WOMEN'S APPAREL.

(From "A New Spring of Divine Poetry," James Day, 1637. Percy Society. Vol. XXVII, p. 143.)

See how some borrow'd off-cast vaine attire,
Can puff up pamper'd clay and dirty mire:
Tell me, whence hadst thy cloaths that make thee fine,
Was't not the silly sheep's before 'twas thine?
Doth not the silk-worm and the oxe's hide,
Serve to maintain thee in thy cheefest pride?
Do'st not thou often with those feathers vaile
Thy face, with which the ostridge hides her taile?
What art thou proud of, then? me thinks 'tis fit
Thou shouldst be humble for the wearing it:
Tell me, proud madam; thou that art so nise,
How were thy parents clad in Paradise?
At first they wore the armour of defence,
And were compleatly wrapt in innocence:
Had they not sin'd, they ne're had been dismaid,
Nor needed not the fig-tree's leavy ayde!
Whatever state, O Lord, thou place me in,
Let me not glory in th' effect of sin.

" Madam, I do as is my duty —
Honour the shadow of your shoe-tie."
—*Hudibras.*

Elizabeth Fry, 1780-1845.

After the portrait by George Richmond, 1824.

CHAPTER V.

THE EVOLUTION OF THE QUAKER BONNET.

Then let Fashion exult in her rapid vagaries ;
  From her fascinations my favorite is free ;
Be Folly's the headgear that momently varies,
  But a Bonnet of Drab is the bonnet for me.

Bernard Barton.

Borrow'd guise fits not the wise—
  A simple look is best ;
Native grace becomes a face
  Though ne'er so rudely drest.

Thomas Campion, 1612.

Martha Routh, 1743-1817.

Silhouette in possession of Charles Roberts, of Philadelphia.

CHAPTER V.

O one brought up within the fold it is no light matter to approach so awful a subject as the Quaker bonnet. There was a certain solemnity about it that was born of terror. Whether it presided at the head of the women's meeting, or ventured in winter storms, protected in its satin or oil-skin case under the Friendly umbrella, or even lay alone in splendid state upon the bed of the welcome guest—anywhere, everywhere, it was a solemn thing. Born of much meditation, constructed with care and skill and many pricks (if not of conscience, at least of fingers *); with time and money and eyesight lavished recklessly upon it, that no deviation of a pleat from the pattern, or tint from the color, or grain from the quality might be wanting— shades of our grandmothers! Can we get our bonnet sufficiently in perspective to realize that it is already a matter of history, that the next generation will know the true Quaker bonnet no more, and that if some of these matters of custom and costume of the past among the Friends are not soon preserved, valuable opportunities for future students of the Quaker will be lost? Let us try.

---

* Plain bonnet-making was a trade exceedingly hard on the fingers.

Again it becomes necessary, in order to study the Quaker headdress, to examine first the worldly bonnet and mode of dressing the hair. The clue to all the changes within the Society may be found without; and not a pleat of the bonnet as now worn by the plainest Friend; not a turn of the shawl, not a flare of the coat nor a roll of the hat-brim, but had its origin at some remote day—let us whisper it softly—in Paris! There was a time when the bonnet, which for the sake of distinction, we shall call Elizabeth Fry's—the " technical " Quaker bonnet, so to speak, known among the irreverent as the " coal-scuttle," or " sugar-scoop," or " stiff-pleat "—was a new thing in America. It came to this country on the head of an accredited English woman Friend, Martha Routh,* who was also a minister; and echoes of its coming had preceded her. A contemporary journal, still in existence, tells us:

Martha Routh, a Minister of the Gospel from Old England, was at Goshen (Pennsylvania) Meeting the 11th. day of 11th. mo. 1798; was a means (if I mistake not) of bringing bonnets in fashion for our leading Frd's, and hoods or Caps on the Cloaks in the Galleries, which of Latter time the Hoods on the Cloaks of our overseers and other active members have increased to an alarming hight or size:—how unlike the dress of their grandmothers! †

What should we not give to behold that same " dress of their grandmothers ! " Martha Routh made a second visit to America in 1802. She writes in her Journal on her return home after her first visit that

---

*Martha Routh, born 1743, died 1817.

†From " A Memorandum Book belonging to Ennion Cook, of Birmingham, Chester county, Pennsylvania," dated 1820. Ennion Cook was the village schoolmaster, and the old memorandum book is in possession of a descendant.

they were taken by a French privateer, when a young
man in the boarding party remarked to her that she
and her women companions looked like the nuns in
France. "I told him," she says, "that we were
Friends or Quakers, and inquired if they had heard of
such in their country? He replied that they had." *
But American Friends have always been more conservative in their dress than their English cousins,
probably because the latter's proximity to the continent forced them into more cosmopolitan habits. At
any rate, American Friends were shocked at the giddy
structure. But time went on. They gazed, they ad-
mired, they stole a furtive pattern; they made the ven-
ture, and behold! When a synonym was wanted for
conservatism, for stability, for all things that endure,
it was found in the Quaker bonnet. How sad that it
must soon be as extinct as the dodo! To understand
the evolution of this bonnet, it is necessary to go back
more than three hundred years, and see through what
changes the worldly bonnet has passed.

The faces of fifteenth century women, declares
Viollet le Duc, were of a uniform type; the prevailing
style of headdress during the Wars of the Roses having a tendency to cause a superficial resemblance
among persons really unlike. Individuality is ob-
scured by the universal adoption of a distinctive effect
in bonnets or gowns. This illusion of similarity is
marked among the few existing portraits of that period,
when the imposing "steeple headdress" was the
mode. That towering structure was composed of rolls
and rolls of long linen, reaching two feet above the

---

* Journal of Martha Routh, p. 280.

head, and going to a point like an extinguisher, from whose apex floated a long gauzy veil. Until the evolution of the Quaker bonnet, no headdress existed lending such uniformity of type to the faces it surmounted, the " commode " and the " high head " not excepted. The " head rail " of the Saxon period, and the " wimple " or " gorget " of Plantagenet times, came down to the early seventeenth century as the hood, with which we shall presently make closer acquaintance. The " head rail " was not shaped at all, but consisted merely of a long piece of linen or stuff drawn over the head like a hood, and loosely wrapped about the neck, the grace of the latter movement, even on the most ungainly, exceeding that of the partly shaped wimple, which was more attractive in early English poetry than in actual life ! The wimple was of silk or white cloth; and when discarded by the women of the period was retained as the " gorget " by the nuns, who to-day may thus trace the origin of the white

1641.

band worn about face and throat, under the black hood.* So universal was the hood that men as well as women wore it; and it remained in general use until the time of Henry VIII.† About 1644, both in France and England, we find again the " coif," usually worn in black, and really another form of hood of crêpe or taffetas, brought forward and tied under the chin.‡ Small bonnets or hoods, with two long " pattes," behind

---

* Hill, " History of English Dress." Vol. I., p. 61.
† See chapter on Hats.
‡ Quicherat, " Histoire de Costume."

the ears, or "mouchoirs" with lace, or "toquets" of velvet (called "bonnets de plumes" because worn with so many plumes), were all tentatively suggesting the coming riot of headdress. A handkerchief of lace fastened with a pin, covered the hair in the time of Richelieu; and the "coif" of deshabille, often called the "round bonnet" ("sans passe ?") became the bonnet after many years seen in the accompanying engraving of the "Fair Quaker." French women of the lower classes, and servants, wore the "coif" with two long "drapeaux" or "bavolettes" streaming down behind—doubtless the origin of the modern "bavolet." English women of the common-alty in the seventeenth century wore broad hats like the men, of beaver, with lower crowns, and caps beneath, tied at the chin. The black beaver hat was also popular for riding. It was not a universal custom with the lower classes at this period to cover the head at all; while shortly after, by way of contrast, Pepys tells us that the aristocracy did

1635.
(From Hollar.)

not remove the hat, even at table. When the wimple was worn under the hat, the latter was fastened on with a hat-pin; so that there is truly nothing new under the sun, not even this modern convenience. At the end of Queen Anne's reign, the revival of the silk trade gave a temporary popularity again to the silk hood. The pointed beaver hat with the cap below, although chiefly a middle-class costume, was in vogue among a few of the plainer in taste of the aristocracy, as may be seen in the portrait of Hester Pooks, second wife of John Tradescant, the younger. She lived from 1608 until 1678; her portrait hangs on the stairway of the Ashmolean Museum at Oxford. She wears a costume exactly similar to the Quakeress Tub-Preacher, including cap and peaked beaver hat, the only difference in dress being the rich lace upon her gown.

This peculiar headdress has remained from the time of James I. (who is responsible for the beaver hat in this form) to the present day among the Welsh women; and almost all of the earliest prints of the Quaker women who preach, show them dressed in this cap and hat. It is impossible, in examining any of these pictures, to avoid the suggestion that here is the hat of the conventional *witch* of our childhood—the old woman, who, for so many years, has swept the cobwebs from the sky; and we are justified in the conclusion. The steeple-

From "Memoires, etc., d'Angleterre." 1698.

crowned hat was worn over the hood about the period between 1650 and 1675; it was popular with the middle and lower classes, and familiar throughout the kingdom. It will be remembered that the terrible witch trials of the Continent, England and Massachusetts in America, all culminated during the latter half of the seventeenth century, the sufferers being chiefly drawn from the class who wore this dress. What more natural and inevitable than that the woman who wore so

The Quakers' Meeting.

About 1648.

After the original engraving by Egbert van Heemskerck.

striking a garb should need but a broomstick to en-
able her to set out as the typical witch, in her journey
to immortality and posterity?* The ideal Quaker
man's garb is that of this period, as seen in the well-
known broad-brim of William Penn, immortalized even
in " Quaker Oats," and on boxes of lye. But the proper
companion for him is the *witch* of story; while, curiously enough, the type of the Quakeress did not crys-
talize until time gave us Elizabeth Fry, a century and
a half later.

Soon after this early period the " City Flat Caps "
became prominent, and were worn by both sexes in a
modified form. The edict went forth that the three-
cornered minever caps for
women should not be worn
by the wives of those who
were not " gentlemen by
descent." † The little black
hood, in the Stuart period,
was getting to be thought
old-fashioned, but its be-
comingness retained it long
in popularity. The large
" capuchins," of which we
read for many years after

Hood Worn by Cromwell's Wife.

this, were riding-hoods, very popular among the
young Quakeresses. It was probably this style of hood
whose strings annoyed the dear men Friends of South-

---

*The high-crowned hats and point-lace aprons in which the " Merry
Wives of Windsor " are often shown, belong properly to the seventeenth
century and not the fifteenth. The pointed hat is still the stock property
of old women to the present day.

† Georgiana Hill, " History of English Dress." Vol. I., p. 226.

wark Meeting, London, in 1707, by dangling down on their heads when hung on the rail above. These " capuchins " were ample enough for storm garments, and, indeed, belonged properly under that head.* The meeting records say:

> It being taken notice of that several women Friends at the Park Meeting do usually hang their riding-hoods on the rail of the gallery, whereby the Friends that sit under the rail of the gallery are incommoded, It's left to Robert Fairman and Mary Fairman to take order for remedying the same.†

The " capuchin " came into this country as a fashionable hooded cloak early in the eighteenth century, and shared its popularity with the smaller " cardinal," a similar garment or hood, so named because the original was of scarlet cloth, like the mozetta of a cardinal. The capuchin (named from its resemblance to the garment distinguishing the monks of that order) was worn by high and low, rich and poor, plain and gay; and the Friends talked unhesitatingly about their " capuchins " and " cardinals," when nothing would have induced them to mention the " heathen " days of the week, or the months of the year! Such things do even " consistent " Friends come to when they seek a literal gospel.

The old hood came with the Pilgrims into New England, and for two centuries was worn by high and low. The subject of covering the head had been receiving the attention of the Puritan divines, and they exceeded

---

* Other varieties of these were, " hongrelines," " cabans," " royales," " balandras," " houppelandes," " mandilles," " roquets," etc. Quicherat, " Histoire de Costume en France," p. 458.

† Beck and Ball, " History of London Friends' Meetings," p. 227.

the Quakers in their notice of such matters. It must
at no time be thought that the Quakers were alone in
their extreme care for the dress
of their constituency. The Puritan clergymen preached more
about bonnets and hats than ever
the Quakers did ; and their
opinions were very varied. For
instance, Mr. Davenport, at New
Haven, preached that the men,
upon the announcement of the
text, should remove their hats
and stand up; Mr. Williams, un-

Cromwell's Time.
(After Repton.)

der whose care was the flock at Salem, Massachusetts,
exhorted the women of his congregation to wear
veils during public worship, quoting Scripture precedent, of course; while a brisk discussion took
place between Cotton and Endicott, at Boston,
on the 7th of March, 1633, at the "Thursday
Lecture," as to whether all women should veil themselves when going abroad. Mr. Cotton argued that, as
by the custom of the place, veils were not considered in
New England a sign of the subjection of women, they
were in this case not commanded by the Apostle.
Endicott took the other side, demanding the proper
covering of the head, particularly in time of worship.
Soon after, at Salem, Cotton preached so effectively,
that one Sabbath day sermon sufficed to convince his
female hearers of the correctness of his attitude, and
the veil did not become customary.*

* Dr. Dexter, "As to Roger Williams," p. 31.

A sumptuary law of James II., in Scotland, ordains, " That noe woman come to the kirk or mercat [market] with her face mussled, that sche may nocht be kend, under the pane of escheit of the curchie." * There were many minds.

The World, a periodical for 1753, contains a letter condemning the ladies for wearing their hats in the churches during divine service, as transgressing against the laws of decency and decorum. At the arraignment of Ann Turner before the King's Bench in 1615, for the murder of Sir Thomas Overbury:

> The Lord Chief Justice told her that women must be covered in the church, but not when they are arraigned, and so caused her to put off her hat; which being done, she covered her hair with her handkerchief, being before dressed in her hair, and her hat over it.†

In 1726, an advertisement in the *Boston News Letter* of September relates the loss of a hood:

> On the Sabbath, the 28th of August last, was taken away or Stole out of a Pew at the Old North Meeting House, A Cinnamon Colour'd Woman's Silk Camblet Riding-Hood, the head faced with Black Velvet.

We are tempted to hope the " cinnamon colour'd woman " got her hood back again ! ‡

The hat was a fashionable rival to the hood, and both men and women alike appeared in felt, beaver and castor hats. The earliest variety of the Puritan hat knew no difference for the two sexes. A " straw hatt " left in the will of Mary Harris, of which Mrs. Earle tells us, was a great rarity in New London in the year 1655, and would have been so equally in London itself

---

* Percy Soc. Vol. XXVII., p. 77.
† Archæologia. Vol. XXVII., p. 61.
‡ W. R. Bliss, " Side Glimpses from the Colonial Meeting-house."

at the same date. We should much like to know what might have been the shape of the " Ladies Newest Fashion White Beaver Riding-Hats," advertised for sale in Boston in 1773. They had been called an "affectation " by all but the ultra-fashionable. Pepys, the ever-watchful, notices one of the earliest hats with commendation. " I took boat again," he says, " being mightily struck with a woman in a hat that stood on the key." * By degrees the tall, steeple-crowned hats became relegated to the country women, and the poorer class in the towns. Ward, speaking of an assembly of " fat, motherly flat-caps," at Billingsgate, says:

> Their chief Clamour was against High heads and Patches; and said it would have been a very good Law, if Queen Mary had effected her design and brought the proud Minks's to have worn High Crowned Hats instead of Top-Knots.†

Elizabeth, the mother of Cromwell, sacrifices no taste to her Puritanism, but wears a handkerchief with broad point lace, and a green velvet " cardinal," the hood just described as affected by the Quaker women. A lady of rank, in Paris, in 1664, is shown in a hood of the same style. Indeed, in these stormy Puritan times, some peo-

Hood Worn by Cromwell's Mother.

---

* Pepys' Diary, June 11th, 1666.

† Misson, *London Spy.* Quoted by Ashton. See also letters of Mme. de Sévigné for a description of her daughter's hair, as arranged by Martin, court hair-dresser.

ple came to regard plain dress as an affectation, put on just as the French ladies at the court of Marie Antoinette all took to playing dairymaid. Still another hood for riding was the " Nithesdale " of the early eighteenth century. No garments were more popular than this and the " cardinal " among the young Quakeresses, as letters of the period testify.

THE RIDING-HOOD.

Let traitors against kings conspire,
Let secret spies great statesmen hire,
Nought shall be by detection got,
If women may have leave to plot;
There's nothing clos'd with bars or locks
Can hinder nightrayls, pinners, smocks,
For they will everywhere make good,
As now they've done the Riding-hood.

Oh thou, that by this sacred wife,
Hast saved thy liberty and life,
And by her wits immortal pains,
With her quick head hast sav'd thy **brains:**
Let all designs her worth adorn,
Sing her anthem night and morn,
And let thy fervent zeal make good,
A reverence for the Riding-hood.*

The song, of which these are the last two stanzas, was composed after the battle of Preston, when Sir William Maxwell, Earl of Nithesdale, and a supporter of the house of Stewart, was taken prisoner. He was tried and sentenced to death. By the skill of his Countess, who disguised him in her dress and large hood, he escaped from the Tower the evening before the sentence was to have been executed, and died in

---

* Percy Society. Vol. XXVII., p. 207.

Rome in 1744. The pluck of the heroic Countess was
celebrated throughout England, and the hood which so
largely contributed to the success of the disguise, became thereafter known as the " Nithesdale."
The " mob " was a rather slovenly undress, always
spoken of disparagingly. There were advertised
" Women's laced Head-Cloths," commonly called
" Quaker's Primers," and " Dowds." * The later tur-
bans of the " Cranford " ladies will at once come to
mind, although this formidable headdress was for elaborate and state occasions as well. A beautiful painting
in the Louvre by Sir Thomas Lawrence of J. Angerstein and his wife, shows the turban at its best. From
the first quarter of the eighteenth century until the
period of the French Revolution, ladies' headdress underwent rapid and appalling changes. A satirical
pamphlet (quoted by Quicherat) names " coiffures à la
culbutte " and " à la daguine "; in 1750 we find them
" en dorlette," " en papillon," " en équivoque," " en
vergette," " en désespoir," " en tête de mouton."
Mademoiselle Duthé is described as wearing " un bonnet de conquête assurée! " Changes were made with
lightning rapidity. A despairing beau in the *London
Magazine*, in April, 1762, wrote:

> Then of late, you're so fickle that few people mind you;
> For my part, I never can tell where to find you!
> Now dressed in a cap, now naked in none,
> Now loose in a mob, now close in a Joan:
> Without handkerchief now, and now buried in ruff;
> Now plain as a Quaker, now all of a puff.†

---

* Ashton, " Social Life in the Reign of Queen Anne," p. 134.
† From " A Repartee," *London Magazine*, April, 1762.

A "Lavinia" unbleached chip hat, trimmed with white sarsenet ribbon, was shown in 1810. The white satin cap underneath was supplemented with an artificial rose in the front of the bonnet. The ladies at this time all talked about the arrangement of their "hind" hair, which was often worn "à la Grecque," the other half into which the "hind" hair was divided, being down the back in fascinating ringlets! Jane Austen, the novelist, wrote

"Lavinia" chip hat for walking; trimmed with white sarsenet ribbon, 1819.

her sister Cassandra from London in 1811:

> I am sorry to tell you that I am getting very extravagant and spending all my money. . . . Miss Burton has made me a very pretty bonnet and now nothing can satisfy me but I must have a straw hat of the riding-hat shape.

Not long before she had written:

> I am quite pleased with Martha and Mrs. Lefroy for wanting the pattern of our caps; but I am not so well pleased with your giving it to them. Some wish, some prevailing wish, is necessary to the animation of everybody's mind; and in gratifying this, you leave them to form some other which will not probably be half so innocent. . . . Flowers are very much worn, and fruit is still more the thing. . . . I cannot help thinking that it is more natural to have *flowers* grow out of the head than *fruit*. What do you think on that subject?*

There were "conversation" or "cottage" bonnets, of straw or chip. The style was really a modified coal-scuttle; "the most fashionable straw bonnets for the

*O. F. Adams, "The Story of Jane Austen's Life," pp. 69–151.

promenade are the *conversation cottage*, which have
have been much distinguished for their negligent neatness! " The " mountain " hat also enjoyed large proportions. In 1808, straw hats and bonnets were only
used in walking or morning costume. In carriage or
evening dress, the hair was worn with veils, flowers,
lace handkerchiefs or similar light attire.

Ann Alexander, an English Friend, who was
in America in 1805, is said by the daughter of
the Friend who was her hostess in this country, to
have taken her bonnet to pieces in order to turn the
silk, when, to the surprise of the American, the English woman's plain bonnet was discovered to have had
a foundation of *straw*.

The " commode," already described, was a pon-
derous headdress, with such a place in history and
literature that its adventures would fill a volume.
Its banishment took a special edict on the part of
Queen Anne.* But the Quakeresses do not seem
generally to have fallen a prey to its enchant-
ments. With its departure it again became possible to dress the hair low. During its reign hats,
which began to appear, some of them in turban shape,
had had no more connection with the head than the
" chapeau bras " of the men. At one time hat *brims*
only were worn to shade the eyes, a whole hat on such
a structure being manifestly a work of supererogation!

But through it all the hood in some form still remained. A popular cap for indoors at this time was the
" fly-cap," in shape like a butterfly, edged with garnets
and brilliants. The ladies at home also wore the " cor-

---

* The name *commode* does not appear to have been used in America.

nette," a little hood with long ends made of a strong
gauze called " marli," or even of baptiste. They were
later the constant wear of the peasant women about and
after 1730. In this class the hood negligé was without
ends. The " bagnolette " was an outdoor protection,

"Cornette."

Composed of tulle,
quilling of blonde
around face, bunch
of flowers on top.
Style is French,
"simply elegant and
becoming"!

October, 1816.

something on this order. In France
it was the " capeline sans bavolet." *
It was really the old coif of Louis
XIV.'s time, worn on the back of the
head, and without anything at nape
of neck. The old cape worn by
elderly ladies became the mantelet.
This was for cold weather, while the
mantilla was a summer garment worn
like a long fichu, thrown over the
head and knotted on the breast. The
mantilla and mantle must not be con-
founded. The latter was often a
large furred pelisse, buttoned from top to bottom
in front, and affording perfect protection. There
were broad-brim straw hats in the early days of
Queen Anne, and for holidays the high-crowned
hat of beaver still had some vogue.† The straw hat
came in as early as the reign of James II. (1685
to 1688), and the hoods for a short time were discarded, to be revived again under French influence
in 1711. Pepys says: " They had pleasure in putting
on straw hats, which are much worn in this country." At this time there was a feeble return to simplicity, and one writer says: " The ladies have been

---

* Quicherat.
† Ashton, " Social Life in the Reign of Queen Anne," p. 248.

moulting, and have cast great quantities of lace, ribbons, and cambric." Swift writes to Stella: "May
19th. 1711; There is a mighty increase of dirty wenches
in straw hats since I knew London." *

It is interesting to note that in America, as long as
the negro women were slaves, they were forced by their
mistresses to wear the bandanna head-handkerchief
as the badge of their servitude. When the Civil War
set them at liberty this detested badge was cast off, and
the many tails and curious knots peculiar to the true
African style appeared, as Mr. Bliss says, " the real inheritance of ancestral taste in chignons, straight from
Guinea! " There were many names for the varieties
of hood in England, for as many years, and the old bal-
lads and broadsides have helped to preserve these.
For instance, " Fine Phillis," printed in 1745, but
much older in date, has the following:

> She's a fine lady,
>   When she's got her things on;
> On the top of her head
>   Is a fine burgogon—
> A crutch there on the side
>   To show her off neat,
> And two little confidants
>   To make it compleat.

The bourgoigne was that part of the headdress near-
est the head—the " crutch " (cruche) and " confidants "
were curls. The hoods were " shabbarons " (chaperon)
and " sorties "; the latter, a walking hood. Cardinals
and capuchins have been described. " Rayonnés " were
hoods pinned in a circle, like sunbeams.

---

* Journal to Stella.

The dress of Anne of Cleves, when brought to England to marry Henry the Eighth, is thus described as to the headdress:

She had on her head a kall [caul] and over it a round bonet or cappe set ful of orient pearle of a very proper fassyion, and before that she had a cornet of black velvet and about her necke she had a partlet set full of riche stones which glistered all the felde.*

The "pinched cap" seems to have been a favorite matter of allusion to characterize the Quaker women by many of the old contemporary writers. Tom Brown, who lived certainly until 1704, and who, of course, had little but derision for the Quakers, says: "What have we here? Old Mother Shipton of the second edition, with amendments; a close black hood over a pinched coif, etc." The "Querpo hood" † worn chiefly by the Puritans and plainer people, was also a Quaker peculiarity after it was discarded by the worldly. Ned Ward, in a dialogue between a termagant and her miserly husband, makes her say:

No face of mine shall by my friends be viewed
In Quaker's pinner and a Querpo hood.

The first mention that Mrs. Earle finds of bonnets in any records of New England is in the year 1725, when two were sent to England in the wardrobe of Madame Usher. By 1743 they were popular, and the middle of the century saw bonnets of many shapes—" Sattin," " Quilted," " Kitty Fisher," " Quebeck," " Garrick,"

---

* Quoted by Repton, Archæologia, XXVII., p. 37.

† " Querpo " was a corruption of the Spanish *Cuerpo*, signifying close fitting. An undress. The body " in querpo "—*i. e.*, in body-clothing—close. See Hudibras :

" Exposed in querpo to their rage
Without my arms & equipage."

The Calash.

Invented 1765.   Worn until about 1830.
From an original photograph.

The Cap.

I. Martha Washington, Silhouette.
II. Amelia Opie, 1769-1853.

*Engraved by Lightfoot, from the medallion done in Paris
by David.*

" Prussian," " Ranelagh," and others. They were of
" plain and masqueraded newest fashion crimson, blue,
white and black." There is no hint of the shapes, un-
fortunately. We are told of the Puritan women in a
certain congregation, that " ye women may sometimes
sleepe and none know by reason of their enormous bonnets. Mr. White doth pleasantlie saye from ye pulpit
hee doth seeme to be preaching to stacks of straw with
men among them ! " In 1769, in Andover, it was
" put to vote whether the Parish Disapprove of the
Female sex sitting with their Hattes on in the Meeting
House in time of Divine Service as being Indecent "
(with a capital I !). The " Hattes " were ordered off,
but with no more effect than if the meeting house had
been a modern theatre!

The calash, invented by the Duchess of Bedford in
1765 was so much more like a buggy-top, or covering to
a gig, both in form and size, that it can hardly be
termed a bonnet, except that to cover the head was its
sole function.

It was made of thin green silk shirred on strong lengths of
rattan or whalebone placed two or three inches apart, which
were drawn in at the neck; and it was sometimes, though seldom, finished with a narrow cape. It was extendible over the
face like the top or hood of an old-fashioned chaise or calash,
from which latter it doubtless received its name. It could be
drawn out by narrow ribbons or bridles which were fastened to
the edge at the top. The calash could also be pushed into a
close gathered mass at the back of the head. Thus, standing well
up from the head, it formed a good covering for the high-dressed
and powdered coiffures of the date when they were fashionably
worn—from 1765 throughout the century; and for the caps worn
in the beginning of this century. They were frequently a foot
and a half in diameter. . . . They were seen on the heads of old

ladies in country towns in New England certainly until 1840 and possibly later. In England they were also worn until that date, as we learn from Mrs. Gaskell's "Cranford" and Thackeray's "Vanity Fair." *

The "punkin" hood was the winter mate to the calash in New England, quilted with rolls of wadding, and drawn tight between the rolls with strong cording. It was very heating to the head.

The caps of the women in this country by the middle of the eighteenth century were in great variety. "Fly caps" appear here also. "Round ear'd caps" had no strings; "strap caps" had a band passing under the chin. A little boy, aged eight years, wrote to his Quaker grandmother:

Burlington, 12 mo. 23, 1833.—Mother wears long-eared caps now, and I think they look better than the old ones. She has worn them a considerable time now, and I have got quite reconciled to the change.

His mother at this time was about thirty-five.

"Bugle fly-caps" were worn in Pennsylvania in 1760. Mob caps are described by Mrs. Earle as a "caul with two lappets," and as we may learn from many old portraits, were much worn. The "mobs" were no doubt the streamers which gave the name to the cap, and their undue length proved a source of uneasiness to the Quakers. The mob cap is most familiar to us in the portraits of Martha Washington, and it is undoubtedly the English original of her cap which furnished the pattern for the familiar type of head dress worn by Elizabeth Fry and Amelia Opie. The milkmaids of London on a May-Day were a sight, in yellow

---

* Alice Morse Earle, "Costume of Colonial Times," p. 72.

and red quilted petticoats, pink and blue gowns, mob caps with lace ends, and flat straw hats with lace lappets, named for Peg Woffington.*

From this time on we find some form of the hat always present. The wide style of hair dressing permitted a lower hat or cap; and at one time fashionable women wore countrified straw hats. Grosley (early George III.) says of Lord Byron's trial: "Many ladies had no other headdress but a riband tied to their hair, over which they wore a flat hat adorned with a variety of ornaments." This hat had a "great effect." "It affords the ladies who wear it that arch roguish air which the winged hat gives to Mercury." † Close caps, ridiculed as "night-caps," literally hoodwinking the wearer, were born in 1773, and three styles of hair dressing are quoted for that year: "A slope bag with no curls, the front toupée brought high and straight; a long bag with about six curls," or "the hair straight with about nine curls crossways." Small chip hats were added. But the universal cap, once worn by young as well as old, was going out; and by June, 1795, at the Royal Birthday festivities not a cap was to be seen. The last hood had disappeared five or six years earlier, and the hat and bonnet had the field. We are told of "bewitching straw hats with open brims tied under the chin, worn in summer; and straw hats so

1786.

---

* Hill, "History of English Dress," Vol. I., p. 182.

† Ibid., Vol. II., p. 50.

round and close as to look like caps, with which dainty little white veils were worn half way over the face." Bonnets had been enormous, the tremendous " poke " having come in with French fashions after the French war. This was the bonnet of which Moore wrote:

> That build of bonnet whose extent
> Should, like a doctrine of Dissent,
> Puzzle church-goers to let it in;—
> Nor half had reached the pitch sublime
> To which trim toques and berets climb;
> Leaving, like lofty Alps that throw
> O'er minor Alps their shadowy sway,
> Earth's humbler bonnets far below,
> To poke through life their fameless way.

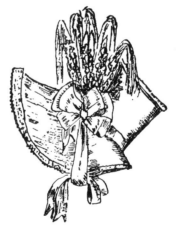

Parisian Promenade Hat. 1816.

Bonnets had fallen back to more decent dimensions after the French revolution, and hats received a round form that justified their Parisian name of " chapeaux casques." *   London still remained for a time the para-

---

* " Le Cabinet des Modes" rejoicingly said, "Nos mœurs commencent à s'épurer : le luxe tombe."

dise of the "high head," and ostrich feathers and plumes had yet a vogue. The bonnet, indeed, had hardly a fair chance, for the towering coiffures made it

1776.

not only unnecessary, but almost impossible. The *Times*, in 1794, says "The ladies' feathers are now generally carried in the sword-case at the back of the carriage." A little later came a paragraph as follows:

There is to be seen on Queen Street a coach on a new construction. The ladies sit in a well, and see between the spokes of the wheels. With this contrivance, the fair proprietor is able to go quite dressed to her visits, her feathers being only a *yard and a half high!*

With the entrance of the nineteenth century came a simpler coiffure, and white satin and black velvet hats were worn on the lowered hair. It was now the ladies' turn to wear hats indoors, and they danced and dined and appeared at functions in their hats, just as they carried white muffs for evening dress. A silver bear muff in 1799, in Philadelphia, cost $14.00, one of grey bear $19.00.

Snuff-taking was not unusual among refined people. There are plenty of references to the old-fashioned Quaker women of the South indulging in a bed-time *pipe,* and we may be sure that the more fashionable " snuffed." In Puritan New England a clergyman held forth against mitts, calling them " wanton, open-worked gloves slit at ye thumbs and fingers for ye purpose of taking snuff ! " Dolly Madison, the favorite and adored of society in America, was an ardent snuff-taker. " You are aware that she snuffs, but in her hands the snuff-box seems a gracious implement with which to charm."

All Paris wore hats indoors. Then came the formidable turban, to which reference has already been made, destined later to become the cap. At this period even young girls wore caps; and up to 1845 " day-caps," with ribbon ends as long as bonnet strings, and tied under the chin, were worn. As the styles seem always to have been calculated for elderly women, it may be fancied what an effect they had on a young face ! The bonnets of 1850 were round and flared wide in front, permitting the cap below to be seen. Then a frill was substituted for the cap, which then and there had its death blow, for the young, at least. England is still eminently the land of caps, so far as the older ladies are concerned. Miss Hill describes " black lace bonnets with a cape or curtain at the back, worn over a hood made of white lawn tied under the chin "—a fashion surviving in the bonnets with white frilled front worn in the middle of the nineteenth century, and still occasionally met with among old-fashioned people.

Fairholt has given us a beautiful old Scotch version of " The Garment of Gude Ladies," belonging to the fifteenth century, which describes such a lady's head-dress as might be the Quaker ideal:

> Would my gude lady lufe me best
> And wark after my will,
> I suld ane garment gudliest
> Gar mak hir body till.*
> Of hê honour suld be hir hud,†
> Upon hir heid to wear;
> Garniest ‡ with governance so good,
> Na demyng suld hir deir.§

It has seemed necessary thus to dwell upon the history of the worldly bonnet, in order the better to follow the progress of that of the Quaker. We may thus trace the succession of the latter's changes. First came the plain hood, together with the pointed high hat surmounting a similar hood; the two styles almost contemporary, and, at least with those not Quakers, often significant of class distinctions. Then came the adoption by degrees, and with many compunctions of conscience, of the hat and bonnet in varying form. The line of descent is quite evident from the time of the " capuchin " and " cardinal " or other form of hood, which among the worldly, served as an outdoor dress in the day of the " high-head," down to the end of the

---

* Cause to be made for her.
† Of high honor should be her hood.
‡ Garnished.
§ No opinion should dismay her—cause her to fear censure. **Percy** Society, XXVII., p. 59.

eighteenth century. The Quakers simply retained it through all the mutations of fashion, until the introduction of the bonnet, the flat hat having kept parallel with it until the evolution of the bonnet of Quakerism in the last century. Why the flat hat should have seemed more plain to the dear Friends, than the small and modest affair at first introduced as the " bonnet," it would puzzle us to determine. But the real bonnet was not accepted by the Friends without many misgivings; and the women of Aberdeen, always careful of the letter of the law, thus cautioned their younger members in the year 1703:

"As touching Bonnets—it is desired that a question be moved at the Quarterly Meeting whether any should be worn, yea or nay." And the meeting thus put itself on record on this momentous question; that " though they might be lawful, it was not expedient to wear them ! " *

Can anything be more delicious than this verdict?

Priscilla Hannah Gurney was one who long retained the old-fashioned black hood, which gave much character to her appearance. So late as 1818, Katherine, daughter of Elizabeth Fry, remembered this ancient Quakeress relative, who had had great influence upon her famous mother. Priscilla Gurney was the daughter of Joseph and Christiana Barclay. She is described as slight in build, and elegant in figure and manner, dressing in the hood, to which reference has been made, long after it had been discarded by others. It is probable that the plain Quaker bonnet has been an evolu-

---

* Minutes of Aberdeen Monthly Meeting, 4 mo., 1703.

tion from the original flat hat of beaver of the middle of the eighteenth century. The bonnet one
degree less plain, with
a square crown, and
gathers, instead of
pleats, would seem to
be the lineal descend-
ant of the peculiar hat-
like bonnet worn by
the " Fair Quaker " of our engraving. It is probably that against which Aberdeen took exception
as " not expedient," and marks a transition period
in bonnets in the world, as well as in the ranks
of Quakerism. But the history of the flat hat is
of great interest. Specimens of these still exist,
and it is from one of these that our illustration
is taken. The thought of putting on the worldly
construction from Paris may have alarmed the plain

18th Century Flat Hat.

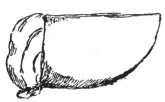

Bonnet of Martha, wife of Samuel
Allinson, of Burlington, N. J.;
died 1823. No strings, one
large box pleat in soft
crown.

Quakeress under her broad
hat a century ago. But who
could have foreseen, in the
dip of the brim that she gave
to her flat hat by tying its
strings under her chin, the
evolution of the present bonnet ? The dip eventually be-
came secured by permanent strings; a soft crown or
cape was added to the resulting cylinder, and the " creation " was complete ! The illustrations are from
contemporary articles, showing the evolution of the

hat into the bonnet, and the change from the first soft crown that was tentatively added to the uncompromising five stiff pleats of the Quaker bonnet in its highest development.

Watson, the annalist of Philadelphia, says: " The same old ladies whom we remember as wearers of the white aprons, wore also large white beaver hats, with scarcely the sign of a crown, and which was confined to the head by silk cords tied under the chin." A recent writer * tells the following tale, which was related to him by an aged relative, to the effect that she remembered " a distinguished female preacher sitting in the ' gallery ' of a country meeting house in summer, with one of these broad, flat, dish-like white beavers on her head, when a cock, flying in through the low, open window, behind the ' gallery,' and perhaps mistaking the hat for the head of a barrel, perched upon it and uttered a vigorous crow ! "

In the year 1786, Ann Warder, who came out at that date from London to join her husband at Philadelphia, went up into the country to attend the funeral of her old friend, Robert Valentine. She was asked, very much to her consternation, to sit in the " ministers' gallery," but made her escape. " I felt so conscious of being higher than I ought to be, intirely among *Cloth Hats*," she wrote, " that I beg'd to return near the Door with the excuse it would be cooler." * Those beaver hats were to the Quaker of the eighteenth century what the plain bonnet, technically so called, has

---

* R. M. Smith, " The Burlington Smiths," p. 157.

† MS. Journal of Ann Warder, 1786–1789.

been to the nineteenth century Quaker. Yet one who should now appear in Arch Street Meeting, Philadelphia, wearing that strange garb of other days would be looked at askance, and hardly admitted into full standing, any more than a certain Irish Friend, who not long since appeared, wearing the dress of William Penn. Indeed, George Fox and William Penn would themselves find a very dubious welcome, if that welcome depended either on their dress or their methods!

A Friend in a Southern Quarterly Meeting in Carolina early in the nineteenth century sent up to Philadelphia, then the center of Quaker fashion, for a black plain bonnet, laying aside her beaver hat. For this proceeding, and its evidence of what the Friends were pleased to regard as her hopeless worldliness, she was severely " dealt with " by the officers of her meeting. There were heart burnings, we may be sure, over bonnets then, even if they were not worldly, and an old family letter written by my grandmother in 1829, says: " —— had a great deal to say on the inroads of fashion, etc., and spoke so particularly as to mention the young women having one kind of bonnet to wear in the streets, and another to meeting. This is very generally the case, I believe." We may be glad to think that the modern young Quakeress has no such temptations to hypocrisy. The same writer adds, a short time later, " A plain young man is hardly to be found anywhere now, and Susan B—— says plain hats are hardly even asked for now. I mean bonnets, for all are called hats here." This was in New York, in 1830.

A painting of Gracechurch Street Meeting, London, about 1778, shows a large assemblage in a pillared hall, whose dignity and dimensions are quite imposing. It is lighted solely from the roof. The men sit on one side, the women on the other, both in rising seats and on the main floor. Some of the women wear the newly-introduced bonnet, like that of the " Fair Quaker," and others wear the flat beaver or " skimming-dish " hat, in some cases tied down over the ears; in others, not. A few of the older women wear hoods. Many of the men are in wigs, and all wear cocked hat, skirt-coat, and knee-breeches. All wear their hats, except the preacher, whose cocked hat hangs on a peg in the wall behind him. Groups of the " world's people " look down upon the worshiping Friends from the galleries above, each group apparently accompanied by a plain Friend who sits with them. This picture is very interesting, as showing the period of transition to the plain bonnet, and fully demonstrating the extent to which the cocked hat and wig were worn among the Quakers during the height of that fashion. It is worth noting that the seats all have the luxury of backs—not a common thing by any means in the meetings of the day.

A Dutch engraving entitled, "Assemblée des Quakers à Amsterdam—Un Quaker qui prêche," shows a plain room lighted from a dome in the ceiling. The hard benches, without backs, are occupied by men in full skirted coats, wigs and cocked hats. They carry enormously long canes, fastened to the wrist by a cord. A few worldly men standing as spectators in the background, wear swords. The hat-brims of two men

Gracechurch Street Meeting,

London, 1776.

Original painting in Devonshire House collection, London.

" The Bride."

From the original in the " Aurora Borealis," published
at New Castle-upon-Tyne, 1833.

Friends are not cocked. The women, plain and gay alike, wear hoods, and many of them crinoline. The date of the picture is much earlier than the preceding. A lovely picture of a young Quakeress, called " The Bride," published originally in the *Aurora Borealis*, a literary annual of Newcastle-upon-Tyne, in the year 1833, shows a sweet young woman in cap and handkerchief, her shawl lightly thrown over her shoulders, and her plain bonnet lying on the table beside her. The cap is an exaggeration of that of Martha Washington, and the bonnet, it will be observed, has a soft crown. That worn by the Queen, in August, 1849, on the Royal Yacht, in Kingston Harbor, has a similar shape, except that it is probable that the Queen's was somewhat stiffened in the crown. Mrs. Lucock, of Beaumont-road, Plymouth, who is 84 years of age, is able to recall with undiminished pride and satisfaction the fact that she once made a bonnet for the late Queen in an early year of her reign. Mrs. Lucock was at the time a young woman employed in a London business which had the orders for the Royal bonnets, the size and shape of which gained for them the name of " coal-scuttles." It is an impressive lesson to one who thinks that the Quakers have cut their clothes by their rule of conscience, and always worn the same style of garment, to examine the cuts and modes in a Parisian fashion journal of 1840-1849, called " Le Conseiller des Dames," from one of which our plate is taken. There our Friend may see the plain bonnet of to-day, exactly reproduced for the ladies of fashion, and worn by Queen Victoria, with only the ostrich plume to betoken any difference existing between Quaker and worldly. The young Quakeresses of the middle of the nineteenth century were given to wearing silk and satin bonnets of very delicate light colors, pearl gray and a rose pink being favorites. The quilled bonnets, and those with a plain front and gathered crown, both now adhered to in Philadelphia, and considered plain, may here be seen in their beginning, and that the modification for every bonnet has had its inspiration in Paris, there seems no possible doubt. It has been with the Quaker bonnet, as with every other garment the Quaker has ever worn:—the cut has originated in that center of all ideas of fashion, and the abode of taste, Paris; while the expression of Quakerism lay simply in the absence of any superfluous adornments. In this one idea lies the secret of Quaker dress. Anything that has tended to pervert this into a uniform, unchanging and arbitrary, has been directly counter to the true spirit of simplicity and meekness which characterized the early Friends.

Sarah Dillwyn, the wife of the well-known Quaker preacher, George Dillwyn, wrote to her sisters in America, upon her arrival in London, early in the year 1784:

My G. D. said he did not wish me to look singular, and my bonnet was much so ... so out she went and bought some nice thin "mode" such as they wear, and made it presently herself; she would have me wear a cloak of hers with a hood, as the plainest of them do. . . . She had on a quilled round hat of gauze, white shade, and I think, a cream-coloured dress, but not so bedizened as I've seen some;—and a little round hoop. The girls did not look tawdry; . . . Neither of them answers George Fox's description; *he paints high!**

---

* J. J. Smith, " Letters of the Hill Family," p. 247.

Queen Victoria.

After an engraving by Freeman. London, 1837.

Fashion Plate, about 1849.

From " *Le Conseiller des Dames,*" *Paris.*

Mary Holgate was a plain bonnet maker in Philadelphia two generations ago. Her finger became injured through making the hard pleats in the bonnet crowns, and she lost the use of her hand. This incident, together with the retirement of the popular bonnet-maker, caused in that city a much greater use of bonnets with the more easily made gathered crowns, since which period these bonnets have received the sanction of the plainest wearers. This style of bonnet has been referred to as the " shun-the-cross." An aged Friend of the latter half of the eighteenth century, when a young girl, promised her father on his death-bed that she would never put on the stiff-pleated plain bonnet, then beginning to be worn, and considered very gay, as our extracts have abundantly shown. She kept her word, and although she was a plain Friend and lived to the great age of ninety-four, she never flinched in her determination to keep her promise, although the flat hat that was the substitute made her very conspicuous, at a period when the stiff-pleat had become correct for the most severe. Finally, after having made a solitary appearance at a certain western meeting for many years, wearing that conspicuous headdress, she determined that she could still keep her promise to her father, and be less conspicuous, by wearing an unconventional bonnet of her own invention. A green lining which she put in it when well advanced in years rather surprised her friends; but she informed them that it was a " relief to her eyes in the sunshine." Her granddaughter had a green wool gown which she feared her grandmother might regard as too gay. When

questioned about it, her grandmother said, " No harm
in wearing green and blue; the grass is green, and the
sky is blue ! " She died in 1857, having moved from
the South to Ohio, then called " Northwest Territory,"
about 1803. Some interesting old Quaker bonnets may
be seen in the collection of ancient garments at the
Museum in Nantucket, Massachusetts. A Quaker bon-

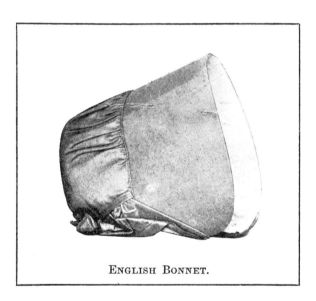

ENGLISH BONNET.

net of black silk, of the date 1728, has small stiff pleats
in the crown; while one of drab, dating from the Revolution, has much larger stiff pleats, showing the development of the present Philadelphia " plain " bonnet,
known in New England as the " Wilburite " bonnet.
There is also in the same collection, one labeled " English " bonnet, distinguished chiefly by a wider flare to

Rainy Day Cover.

From an original photograph.

the front. The English bonnets seem always to have
had a shorter front, and a wider flare at the face; in
fact, to have had a much more sensible shape, if comfort was to be considered at all, as it evidently was not
in America! Nothing more dangerous could have
been devised for an elderly person whose sight or hearing was somewhat defective than the long tunnel sides
of the pasteboard front of a plain bonnet of the nineteenth century.

Ann Warder, whose journal has already been
quoted, was remonstrated with by an intimate friend
for wearing a " whalebone " bonnet, because of its
greater worldliness than one of pasteboard, as the early
plain bonnets were always called. We should be glad
to know what the condemned bonnet was like. Quite
probably the lining was of some bright color, and the
" casing " or " drawn " bonnet is no doubt its natural
successor. Apropos of the " pasteboard " bonnets, we
may read in *Poulson's Daily American Advertiser*
for Saturday, August 23d, 1828, among the Philadelphia advertisements, the following notice: " Bonnet-
boards—50 groce of good quality at a low price, and a
few groce of fine quality." They were for sale by
James Y. Humphreys, at 86 South Front Street.
Doubtless these were the foundations, for the fronts of
both worldly and plain bonnets consisted of pasteboard
forms, over which the silk or other covering was
stretched, resulting in the " poke " or the " coal-scuttle " as might happen. The same interesting Warder
Journal, which went in instalments to an English sister
in London, has the following entry:

September, 1788. [Ann Warder had no dread of the "heath-
en" names of the months.] I put no cloak on this forenoon, but
was obliged to afterward, not to look singular, for some had long
ones lined with Baize down to there toes, but no hoods, instead
of which a lay-down coular [collar] which would look very dis-
agreeable to me but for the Cape to there Bonnets, hiding the
neck. Black are worn more here than with us;—no Brown except Cloth.

This was at Yearly Meeting time, then in the au-
tumn, to prepare for which she had written just before:

9mo. 22.—This forenoon I sat pretty close to my needle, in
some degree preparing for Yearly Meeting, wishing to want nothing in the Cap or Apron way that week.

The thieves that she mentions as having broken into
the house during the previous week, made off, among
other things, with " a new white Myrtle gown, a petticoat, apron, boots, J's new white hat and two old ones."
The " Cape to there Bonnets, hiding the neck," was
that of the " wagon " bonnet, so called from its resemblance to the top of a " Jersey " wagon; they were
usually of black silk, and had a pendant piece of the
same from the back of the bonnet, covering the shoulders. The " wagon " bonnet antedated the " coal-
scuttle," still lingering among us. It was the style
worn by Rebecca Jones, of Philadelphia, the friend of
John Woolman.

But the plain bonnet had its intricacies, and it is
not for the stranger to learn them in a day. Like the
stars, one bonnet differeth from another in glory.
Eventually, modifications of the extreme conservative
crept in; and we have the popular close bonnet, with
fine gathers rather than pleats, and a shorter front,
which allows itself a furtive bow under the square

crown, and which is found in the more modern shades of blacks and browns, rather than the original drabs and grays, called long ago by an irreverent young Friend, the " shun-the-cross " bonnet. It daily grows harder to discern social differences in congregations by means of the once infallible test of hats and bonnets. Even among the worldly, the distinction of class dress

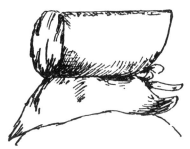

Bonnet from doll model of costume of Rebecca Jones, of Philadelphia; died 1817. Dressed by "Sally Smith," of Burlington, N. J. Soft gathered crown, large cape with three points—one on each shoulder and one in center of back.

is nearly or quite obliterated. It is therefore a surprise to find a sect in Pennsylvania who " disown " at the present day for gaiety of attire—a thing not known now among Friends for many years.*

The plain bonnet, too, has had its romance. In the

---

* *The Public Ledger* for November 1, 1899, had the following remarkable notice :

"BARRED FROM CHURCH BY HAT

" Miss May Oller, of Waynesboro, . . . who lately returned from a trip to the Holy Land, has been expelled from the Antietam German Baptist Dunkard Church for discarding the plain bonnet for a pretty creation of the milliner's art. At a meeting of the church authorities in July, Miss Oller was notified that she must return to the wearing of the bonnet, and that she would be given until October to put away her hat. . . . Although the defence was set up that the annual meeting had made the wearing of a hat or bonnet discretionary, Miss Oller's expulsion was ordered by a large majority. . . . Miss Oller is the daughter of the late Bishop Jacob F. Oller."

days when it concealed youth and beauty, and the broad-brim had to bend, in order to see within its depths, hearts were warm and faces gay, even in sober garb; and the old story was whispered just the same in the long tunnel of the bonnet. The little street urchins were once said to have chased a beautiful Quakeress some distance down the street of one of our great cities, in order to run around in front and peep up at the lovely laughing eyes that met their admiring glances. One young bride is said to have threatened to cut a slit in the side of her bonnet, in order to be able to see her new husband when driving beside him on their way to meeting! Are we not to suppose that his sentiments might have been those of the Quaker friend of Wendell Phillips, as he sat quietly thinking to himself:

> My love's like a red, red rose
> That's newly blown in—*the Sixth Month!*

Then, too, the crashing kiss of two full-fledged Quaker bonnets is something awe-inspiring to contemplate. The bonnets collide at top speed; occasionally they have been known to telescope, when the rescue is effected by a third party. The usual result, however, is to send each bonnet far back on the head of the wearer, since the front projects some inches beyond the face —when a necessary pause for readjustment follows, infinitely funny to a spectator blest with a sense of humor.

Now the Quaker philosophy of costume is essentially in the direction of plainness and moderation. But the study we have been making shows us how contrary to the true spirit of Quakerism the technical bonnet, for instance, really is. Adopted in the days of decadence of spirituality, when life was easy, and time permitted infinite attention to details, the bonnet became literally a snare, a fetish, a sort of class distinction, at one time almost as exclusive in its work as the mark on the forehead of the high caste Brahmin. That day is effectually past; the modern Quakeress has now but the tradition to preserve of the outward shell, and must address herself to far greater moral problems. She must, nevertheless, like Charles Lamb, who loved the Quakers, endeavor to " live up to that bonnet."

Politics and religion have alternately determined the style of women's headdress. In the days of Charles James Fox, the women of his way of thinking wore a fox tail in the hat or bonnet. To-day, as we pass along the street, the nun, the Quaker, the Dunkard, and the Salvation Army girl are the only types left where the doctrine of the wearer may be read at a glance. To the initiated, the Quaker bonnet once spoke volumes; a glance sufficed to distinguish Beaconite, Wilburite, Maulite, Gurneyite, or Hicksite, and the dwellers in the Mesopotamia of the East. But time has leveled distinctions here as elsewhere ; and manifestations of doctrinal difference are sought to-day, with more regard for truth, in the heart rather than on the head.

The venerable Margaret (Fell) Fox, eight years after her husband's death, raised her voice in warning against legal conformity, seeing in the society for which she had done and suffered so much a tendency

altogether contrary to the spirituality of the Gospel.
From her published epistles we extract the following:

Legal ceremonies are far from Gospel freedom; let us beware of
being guilty or having a hand in ordering or contriving what is
contrary to Gospel freedom; for the Apostles would not have
dominion over their faith, but be helpers of their faith. It is a
dangerous thing to lead young Friends much into the observation
of outward things, which may easily be done, for they can soon
get into an outward garb to be all alike outwardly, but this will
not make them true Christians.

Epistle from M. Fox to Friends, 4 mo., 1698.

"Wilburite."   1856.   "Gurneyite."

INDEX.

Aberdeen 21, 140, 214
Advices 4
Alexander, Ann 203
Amsterdam 218
Angerstein 201
Anne, Queen 10
Apron 133-137
" Aurora Borealis " 219
Aylmer 81

Bavolette 193
Bodice 140
Bolton, John 146
Bonaparte, Prince 168
Bourgoigne 205
Brissot 159
Brown, Moses 107
Budd, Rachel 161

Cadenette 101
Calash 207
Calico 169
Callowhill, Hannah 130
Camlet 41
Cane 16, 17
Canons and Institutions 75
Cap 182, 208, 209
Cape 224
Capuchin . ... .124, 196, 213
Cardinal 57, 196, 213
Carpet 23
Casing (Bonnet) 223
Castor 59
Cathcart, Lady 106
Cavalier 10
Chalkley, Thomas 139
Chapeau Bras 66
Charles I. 16, 102, 104, 112
Charles II. 68, 73, 95
Charlotte, Queen 130
" Chronicle," London 33
Classicism 167
Claypoole, James 146

Clergy 8, 94, 197
Cleves, Anne of 206
Clogs 153, 179
Coach 98
Coal-scuttle bonnet 190
Coat, Skirt 32
Cocked hat 63-65
Collar 16, 36, 117
Collins, Isaac 161
Colonists 39, 106
Color 30, 31, 132, 133, 158
Comb 145
Commode 142, 144
Coif 192,193
Congénies 152
Conscience 54
" Conseiller des Dames " 219
Conservatism 3
" Conversation " bonnet 202
Cookworthy, William 71, 79
Cornette 204
" Cottage " bonnet 202
Cotton, John 197
Cranmer 9
Crinoline 137
Cromwell, Elizabeth 199
Cromwell, Oliver 15

Dartmouth 42, 107, 108
Davenport, John 197
Dickinson, Mary 158
Dillwyn, George 71
Dillwyn, Sarah 137, 166, 220
Dillwyn, William 99
Doll 150, 151, 152
Doublet 16, 39, 40, 41
Dragoon 32
" Drawn " bonnet 223
Drinker, Elizabeth 111, 164
Drummond, May 134, 135
Dublin 21, 109
Dunkard 227
Dutch 158

Edwards, Jonathan 144
Eliot, John 106
Ellwood, Thomas . . 12, 19, 84, 86, 102
Embroidery 29
Emlyn, John 1, 93, 149
Endicott, Governor 106, 197
English bonnet 222
Everett, John 103
Extravagance 9

Falbala [" furbelow "] 97
Fan 153, 154
Fashion " babies " 150
Feathers 211
Fell, Margaret 124
Fell, Sarah 125
Felt 58, 59
Fichu 140
Flat cap 195
Flat hat 214, 215
Fothergill, Dr. 71, 99
Fox . . .10, 14, 16, 18, 68-70, 75, 76, 96
Franks, Rebecca 164
Fry, Elizabeth 4, 174, 184

Gardens 24
Gay 49
Germans 94
Gorget 192
Gracechurch 218
Greaton [Father] 9
Grellet, Stephen 103, 151
Gurney, Hannah 159
Gurney, Joseph John 89
Gurney, Samuel 89
Gurneys 173-177

Handkerchief 128, 140
Hanway, Jonas 49
Headdress 213
Headrail 192
Heart breaker 143
Heels 34
Henrietta Maria 147
Henry (Prince) 62
Henry VIII. 98, 206
Hetherington, John 72
Hogarth 20
Holgate, Mary 221
Hood.104, 193, 195-6, 198, 203, 205, 214
Hoop 137
Humphreys, James Y. 223

James I. 194
James II. 74, 198
Jefferson 39
Jeffersonian coat 39
Jones, Owen 71
Jones, Rebecca 151, 171, 224
Jonson, Ben 112
Jordan, Richard 88

Keith, Sir William 78
Kevenhuller 65
Kinsey, John 78
Kirkbride, Jonathan 41
Kneel 75
Kossuth 67

Lace 16
Lamb 38
Lampoon 25, 28
Lappet 209
Latey, Gilbert 20
" Lavinia " chip hat 202
Lay, Benjamin 43
Lay, Sarah 44
Leather 17, 31
Lettsom, Dr. 71, 99
Levite 166
Limoges 151
Lloyd, Thomas 158
Lloyds 38
Logan, Maria 158
Louis XIV. 34
Lovelock 143
Lower, Thomas 128

Macy, Reuben 74
Mandillions 40
Mantelet 204
Mantilla 204
Marie Antoinette 150
Mason, Martin 77
Massachusetts 104
Meade, William 78
Mennonites 11
Methodist 144
Minever 195
Mirror 63, 64
Mitts 180
Mode 183
Model 150
Montague 76
Montero cap 84, 86, 87
Mott, Richard 42

Mouchoir 192
Moustache 94
Mucklow, William 76
Muff 35, 212
Mulliner, John 112

Nantucket 43, 108
Napoleon 101
Nayler, James 9, 93
Needham, Ann 82
Negro 205
Newlin, Nathaniel 49
Nightgown 146
Nithesdale, Earl of 200
Nollekins 136
Nonconformity 123
Norris, Isaac 158
Nugent 102
Nuns 192

Overbury, Sir Thomas 198
Overcoat 42
Overseers 22

Pantaloons 37
Pantelets 116
Paris 190
Parton, James 94
Pasteboard 223
Patten 179
Patterson, Elizabeth 168
Pattes 192
Pembertons 71
Penn, Hannah 71
Penn, Thomas 71
Penn, Sir W. 62
Penn, William 16, 67, 78, 158, 184, 195
Pennsylvania 105
Pepys 100, 102, 106, 149
Periwig 97
Perot, John 77
Peter the Great 96
Petition 79
Petticoat 137
Phelps, N. 82
Philadelphia 108, 110, 152, 159
Physician 46-48
Pilgrim 40, 74
Pinched cap 206
Pinners 153
Plaid 131
Plume 62, 63

Points 17, 104
Poke 209
Poulson's Advertiser 223
" Precisions " 103
Presbyterian 28, 29, 76
Proud, Robert 71
" Punkin " hood 208
Puritan 12, 29, 73-4,
    94, 104, 106, 119, 157, 197, 207

Querpo 206
Queue 66, 101
Quilled bonnet 220

Reel 131
Reticule 166
Revolution 163
Richardson, Richard 114
Richelieu 193
Riding hat 199
Riding hood 155, 200
Rilston 141
Rochefoucauld, de la 159
Rock 131-2

Safeguard 155
Sandwich 107
Savery, William 174
Saxton 98
Sewall, Judge 106
Shackleton, Richard 137
Shad 36
Shattuck, Samuel 82
Shawl 171
Shepard, Hetty 106
Shippen, Edward 49
Shirt 116
Shoe-strings 34
" Short gown " 139
" Shun-the-Cross " bonnet 221
Sleeves 180
Snuff 153, 212
Springett, " Guli " 129, 159
Starch 116
Stays 150, 182
Steeple hat 60, 199
Steeple headdress 191
Stiff pleat 190
Stockings 38
Stomacher 138
Story, Thomas . ..13, 48, 87, 96, 147
Straw 198, 203, 204, 209

232   *INDEX.*

Stuarts 10
Stubbes 145, 149, 156
Subscription hat 59
Suffolk 102
Sugar-scoop 190
Sumner [Archbishop] 95
Surtout 42
Suspenders 48
Swarthmoor 125
Swift, Dean 67, 134, 205
Sword 32, 63

Taber, Thomas 107
Talbot, Richard 48
" Tatler," The 5
Tea 23
Testimony 89
Tillotson, Archbishop 95
Tobacco 24
Toleration 7
Tomkins, Mary 83
Top hat 66, 74
Toquet 192
Trade 22
Tradescant, John 194
Trousers 36
Trunk hose 37, 40
Tub preacher 128, 194
Tucker, John 107
Turban 144, 201
Turner, Anne 198
Type 6, 184

Umbrella 48, 49, 50
Underclothing 168

Vane, Sir Henry 70
Verney, Sir R. 50
Victoria, Queen 219
Viollet le Duc 191
Vizzard 156

" Wagon " bonnet 224
Waln, Nicholas 48
Warder, Ann—
    47, 110, 155, 165, 178, 216, 223
Washington, George 66, 101
Washington, Martha 208
Watson, John 216
Weaver 132
Wedding 161, 162
Welsh 194
Wesley, John 14
Whalebone 223
Wharton, Edward 83
Whisk 126, 140
Whitall, Ann 160
Whitall, John M. 34
White, Rev. Mr. 207
Whitehead, George 76
Wickes, Rev. George 111
Wig 16, 33, 47, 95, 98
" Wilburite " bonnet 222
Williams, Rev. Mr. 197
Wilson, John 82
Wimple 192, 193
Witch 194
Woolman, John 50-52

York 141